The Critical Few

The Critical Few

Energize Your Company's Culture by Choosing What Really Matters

Jon Katzenbach with James Thomas and Gretchen Anderson

In Collaboration with
the Katzenbach Center Community of Practice

Berrett–Koehler Publishers, Inc.
a BK Business book

Berrett-Koehler Publishers, Inc.
1333 Broadway, Suite 1000
Oakland, CA 94612-1921
Tel: (510) 817-2277
Fax: (510) 817-2278
www.bkconnection.com

ORDERING INFORMATION
Quantity sales. Special discounts are available on quantity purchases by corporations, associations, and others. For details, contact the "Special Sales Department" at the Berrett-Koehler address above.
Individual sales. Berrett-Koehler publications are available through most bookstores. They can also be ordered directly from Berrett-Koehler: Tel: (800) 929-2929; Fax: (802) 864-7626; www.bkconnection.com.
Orders for college textbook / course adoption use. Please contact Berrett-Koehler: Tel: (800) 929-2929; Fax: (802) 864-7626.

Distributed to the U.S. trade and internationally by Penguin Random House Publisher Services.

Berrett-Koehler and the BK logo are registered trademarks of Berrett-Koehler Publishers, Inc.

Printed in the United States of America

Berrett-Koehler books are printed on long-lasting acid-free paper. When it is available, we choose paper that has been manufactured by environmentally responsible processes. These may include using trees grown in sustainable forests, incorporating recycled paper, minimizing chlorine in bleaching, or recycling the energy produced at the paper mill.

Cataloging-in-Publication Data is available at the Library of Congress.
ISBN: 978-1-5230-9872-9

First Edition
25 24 23 22 21 20 19 18   10 9 8 7 6 5 4 3 2 1

Book producer and editor: PeopleSpeak
Text designer: Marin Bookworks
Cover designer: Jennifer Meyers

To all those we love, whose support we rely on,
and especially to the memory of Linda Katzenbach

Contents

Foreword

Transformation used to be something that companies did only in extraordinary circumstances. But today, transformation is something that business leaders have to contend with almost constantly. In a world of rapid technological change, global convergence, increasing external scrutiny, and competition for top talent, all management is now change management.

Executives have come to appreciate the importance of having the right organizational culture to thrive in the new reality they are creating. That is the focus of the latest book by our colleagues at the Katzenbach Center within PwC, Jon "Katz" Katzenbach, James Thomas, and Gretchen Anderson. The book doesn't promise a secret formula or magic wand to create the ideal organizational culture. Instead, a series of reflections, ideas, and tools are offered to equip executives to use the culture they've got as a catalyst for meaningful change within their organization.

The key to doing so, Katz and his coauthors say, is to start small: you don't need a hundred ideas about who you are but a very narrowly focused group.

For example:

- A company has many traits, but only a few are vital symbols of the new enterprise you're trying to become.
- A company has many behaviors, but only a few represent the path forward that everyone needs to follow.

- A company has hundreds or thousands of decision-makers, but cultural transformation starts by targeting and harnessing the energies of a select, special—sometimes unconventional—few.

Crucially, the book argues that each organization's culture already contains the components it needs to fuel successful transformation, and leaders effect lasting, positive cultural change by encouraging behaviors that promote those elements. You don't need to replace your old culture; you need to find the aspects of it that can help you move forward.

What's interesting is not only the insights this book delivers but how it does so: not as a set of rules but as a conversation. Literally, *The Critical Few* presents an ongoing discussion between Katz and "Alex," a fictional CEO who's a composite of the many business leaders the authors have engaged with over the years. Many readers will recognize themselves in Alex and find themselves rooting for him and Katz to succeed in their work of harnessing culture to turn Alex's company around.

The core message of cultural evolution has powerful resonance for us at PwC in our own journey toward even better alignment and collaboration across our global network of firms. This book has amplified my appreciation of the power of our own organizational values and culture, and how we can work better together to have a positive impact on those we interact with and serve.

The Critical Few has real emotional resonance. No company is purely rational. The culture is where its collective emotions reside, and this book shows what's required to reach those emotions: Clarity. Simplicity. Connection.

Our journey at PwC has been enriched by working with the Katzenbach Center since it joined our network as part of Strategy& in 2014. I am confident that business leaders at all levels within their organizations, and from all manner of organizations around the world, will find much to inspire them in the pages that follow.

Bob Moritz
Global Chairman, PwC

Letter to Readers from the Katzenbach Center Community of Practice

Dear Reader,

By virtue of our common interest, we have all one by one found our way into this "club"—the coterie of people within our firm who share ideas, collaborate, argue about the fine points of *mind-sets* versus *behaviors*, and generally boost and enhance one another's knowledge and passion for the topic of organizational culture.

Welcome to our community!

We want to add our voice to that of the coauthors and to encourage you to apply this approach to your daily work. The "critical few" methodology is one that we have practiced, as a whole or in parts, in client situations across industries and around the globe. We all stand behind it: it works! And we encourage you in your own research, writing, and work with others to make practical use of these ideas. We trust that you will see a real benefit, and we look forward to hearing about it.

At the end of the book, you will find a biography for each of us. Enjoy reading this book, and please stay in touch.

DeAnne Aguirre	Michelle Kam
Reid Carpenter	Per-Ola Karlsson
Varya Davidson	Paolo Morley-Fletcher
Diana Dimitrova	Carolin Oelschlegel
Kate Dugan	Frédéric Pirker
Jaime Estupiñán	Roger Rabbat
Amanda Evison	Barry Vorster
Kristy Hull	Alice Zhou

Prologue

My name is Jon Katzenbach, and the book you hold in your hands is the product of five decades spent writing, talking, obsessing, and most of all doing *real work* with clients and colleagues related to the topic of organizational culture. Over the course of these decades, I've had countless conversations like the ones around which this book is structured. I have worked hand in hand on real client situations with the Katzenbach Center Community of Practice, and together we have crystalized these ideas into a methodology and brought it to life in client situations. And for the past few years, I have worked hand in hand with my coauthors, James Thomas and Gretchen Anderson, to bring these ideas and methods to life on these pages.

The framework of this book is a year in the life of a newly minted CEO named Alex. Alex and his company, the Intrepid Corporation, are fictitious. However, Alex is a credible composite drawn from deep conversations and working relationships with countless flesh-and-blood leaders—real individuals who have trusted me with their deepest hopes and fears about their organizations.

James, Gretchen, and I chose to feature the fictional Alex rather than any of these specific individuals or companies for two reasons. First and foremost, this approach helps us to convey how common and universal cultural challenges are, how familiar they feel from organization to organization.

Second, the choice reflects how intimate and personal each company's culture issues are. Aligning culture always involves getting to the heart of difficult matters, unearthing the "family secrets" of a company—the emotional histories that lie under the surface of the story the company tells about itself to the outside world. Our clients speak to us with trust; we treat their issues with discretion.

This is how we run our business, but it creates a unique challenge in writing a book! We intend to convey a real sense of how practical and hands-on any intervention in a company's culture can and should be, and simultaneously we hesitate to display the family secrets we've learned over the years. Thus, for this book, we've chosen a hybrid approach of fact and semifiction. Each chapter opens with a dialogue between Alex and me, a fictional construct that echoes the kinds of conversations I've had with leaders over the decades when they've come to me seeking counsel on how to catalyze real shifts in how people think, believe, and, most importantly, behave. Each dialogue is then followed by a theory-and-practice section that illustrates the ideas that Alex and I discuss using real examples, some from our experience and some from the public domain, and offers practical tips for how to take these concepts forward in your own company.

Intrepid, the company Alex leads, is identified as a retail company. We made this choice because retail is a type of business familiar to just about every reader. But we've deliberately kept the description of the business to a minimum because this tale could just as easily have been set at an airline, an automaker, a bank, a life sciences company, an energy company, or a telecom provider. Over the years, we've served clients in all these industries and many more. We also see the culture challenges that resemble those of Intrepid at government, public, and military institutions, and at non-profit organizations. Professional services firms (our peers and other types of advisors, such as lawyers) are also not immune. The challenges that arise with managing cultures to support and enable the strategic goals of the overall enterprise do not discriminate.

Every industry (and indeed, every company or global institution) has its own unique cultural situation, but all organizations have one thing in common. Whenever they summon the collective will to commit to meaningful change, the success or failure of this effort depends on whether and how they choose to engage their organizational culture. And increasingly, "committing to change" is not a one-time occasion or event but a constant challenge of twenty-first century management. Eighty percent of respondents to our Katzenbach Center global survey on culture believe that their organization must evolve to succeed, grow, and retain the best people, and every client we visit talks about "the constancy of change" and "change fatigue." So the question of just how to guide and catalyze this constant evolution really is the problem that every leader needs to solve. So let's say it again, in another way. If you are a leader at any level and you see an opportunity to move your business in a new direction, you will be far more successful if you engage your culture in your effort. Conversely, if you ignore your culture or presume that it will resist you, you will be far less likely to achieve your goals. Consider the following business challenges.

Broadly speaking, any type of *transformation* has, at its heart, the imperative that people within a company must begin to act and deliver in new ways. To make this ask of your workforce, you need to consider emotional engagement—the basic concept that is at the heart of our approach to cultural intervention.

If a company is looking to reduce costs, to invest in differentiated capabilities or improve profitability or, in the term we use within our own firm, become *"fit for growth,"* emotions will run high. No company in history has ever managed a reduction in resources or workforce reskilling without triggering feelings of loss, fear, or skepticism. In this context, a culture-led approach can help leaders acknowledge and address those emotions—and even more significantly, be sure that cost containment is done in a manner that addresses and acknowledges the behavioral element intrinsic to any major change. This is the real key to sustainable, lasting cost reduction and investment in capabilities—not just removal of costs but prevention so they don't creep back in.

In the broad category of changes referenced now as the *workforce of the future*, companies have begun to look ahead and adapt their structures and ways of working to align with anticipated trends, such as automation of tasks, robotics, and new ways of experiencing the built environment. These types of changes require embedding new capabilities. Often, companies are disappointed to discover that their workforce isn't prepared to realize these and other future-focused opportunities. Transformation then is viewed as a steep uphill battle instead of an opportunity to catalyze the natural cultural elements that would reinforce and inspire change.

Risk and regulatory issues demand culture solutions as well. Consider a company whose strategy must shift to accommodate emerging trends in policy and regulation. Its leaders would be well served by not just dictating top-down changes to process but by taking a holistic look at how employee behaviors either amplify or reduce the risk of noncompliance. Similarly, in the realm of *taxes*, new legislation, just like new policy and regulation, often catalyzes the need for changes to an organizational structure. Anytime boxes are moved in an organizational chart, people are impacted, so culture must be considered. This is especially true today, when investors and auditors no longer tolerate long-held practices such as shell corporations for tax purposes but require transparency and proof points to back up any company's claim of good corporate citizenry.

Finally, if a company is considering a *deal or acquisition*, culture can make or break its success. It's never too early to start to consider culture in the context of a deal—for the most forward-looking companies and private equity firms, culture diagnostics are now considered essential to due diligence. Beyond these early assessments, we believe that a number of questions should drive any integration, such as, What are the qualities that the two companies have in common? Are we prepared to accentuate them? Where are the sharpest divergences? How will we reconcile them—and what might get lost if we do? What are the emotional triggers that might either catalyze integration or stand in the way? Who are the individuals on both sides whom others will look to for energy and support during the most stressful moments, and how can we prepare those people to work together from the early stages to ensure a smoother road?

A powerful common thread links these scenarios. When there is a big change to make, a change of any type, powerful emotional forces in the organizational culture seem, at first blush, to resist it. Under the surface, however, *other* emotional forces are also brewing and multiplying. And these forces are potential sources of catalytic strength. The best leaders succeed by looking past that first inertia or resistance and tapping those sources of strength, as well as resisting the urge to drown simple emotional truths in rational argument and theoretical complexity. This, in a nutshell, is the fundamental lesson of this book, the "secret" I will reveal if you lend me your attention and turn through these pages. Positive emotions matter enormously and can energize any effort. People must feel good about what is asked of them— and the only way to evolve their behaviors is to help them attach positive emotions to the (inherently frightening) idea of any kind of change.

Another secret is that what leaders first perceive as resistance or inertia might be a pace of change that isn't yet visible to the naked eye. The best leaders know that changing a culture takes real time and are adept at ferreting out and rewarding what is evolving, rather than throwing their hands in the air and despairing about how their organization is "stuck." The best leaders also know that looking at the organization only at the surface, as a totality, provides an incomplete picture and can consider their company as a morass of subcultures, competing with and catalyzing and rubbing against each other. There is no such thing as a monolithic culture within any global enterprise or large institution: most institutions of any size are, by definition, multicultural.

Cultures can change, but real change is slow unless you undertake a focused intervention. Subcultures exist in any enterprise and can be powerful sources of emotional identification, but an enterprise-wide culture exists as well and has its own emotional power. These and other paradoxes are at the heart of understanding how to manage your organization's culture. This book aims to teach you how to recognize the emotions and relationships of the enterprise, as well as their local differences, and the effect they have on your strategy and execution capabilities.

If you really want to change your company, you'll need a high level of empathy, great persistence and resolve, rigorous focus, and a practical methodology that brings out the best in your current cultural situation. You'll need something like the critical few. That's what our composite CEO-hero, Alex, discovers in the course of this book.

I've now done quite a bit of talking. Thanks for sticking with me so far. As you'll learn if we someday have the pleasure of meeting in person, for someone who founded a firm and a knowledge center in his own name, I don't love to hold center stage—I much prefer to listen. So I'll step back here and let Alex introduce himself.

—Jon Katzenbach

MEET ALEX

I have always been too ambitious and ambivalent to be easily satisfied. According to my parents, it was easy to picture me making a difference in the world. I was also more pragmatic than academic. When I was a high school student, my ambitiousness kept my grades high enough to capture teachers' attention, but I always knew that I was looking for a broader perspective than schoolwork offered. I got into the habit of stopping by after class to ask my teachers questions—not about the assignments but about life in general. What does someone need to do to get a good job after school? How smart do you have to be? Why do some people turn out well and others fail? And why are some of the most likeable people less successful?

There were always one or two teachers who made time for me. As I got older, my questions grew more sophisticated. And the answers were more interesting. I went on to college, where I studied economics and minored in psychology and computer science. I joined a dot-com right at the tail end of that trend; then, like many of those left scrambling when the bubble burst, I went right on to business school. As the years progressed, my ambitions grew broader. Like many of my B-classmates, I wanted it all—the opportunity to lead, a comfortable living, and the potential to make an impact in some important way. We all understood that the world was rapidly becoming more interconnected and complex. This both frightened and exhilarated us. I felt separate from the others, though. While they seemed to think that their first job after business school would set their path for life, it felt crystal clear to me that many of the old rules no longer applied. I knew that my first job would not be the end-all but just the first step in a much longer journey. I credit this long view to the many conversations I'd had with older advisors over the years.

After business school, I joined a small strategy consulting firm. Jon Katzenbach, one of the firm's founders and the "name on the door," was short and bespectacled, a cycling enthusiast with an unflappable demeanor. Nobody in the firm, from fellow partners to admins to tech support, ever called him "Mr. Katzenbach"—he was only "Katz." He'd been a partner at one of the premier global management consultancies, where he'd specialized in helping companies in a wide swath of industries navigate from startups to behemoths. Then he'd focused his attention on what he called "leading between the lines," the informal relationships that made a company and team really work. He knew a lot about strategy: picking a market, channeling investments to win, establishing the right team at the top, and getting the metrics right.

But his real passion was in helping companies figure out how to encourage people to behave in ways that aligned with their company's mission. It was Katz who helped me see the real human need that every individual in a company has for feeling that his or her work contributes in some way to a larger whole—and how often leaders fail to speak to and make use of this need. Katz called this "obtaining emotional commitment versus rational compliance." As my peers and I worked with Katz and his partners, we learned some of those insights and skills ourselves. Our commitment to that firm and each other was intense: to this day, some of my closest confidants, the ones I'll call on for help and advice for both personal and professional challenges, are friends whom I met in that firm.

Even with as little actual work experience as I'd had at that time, it was clear to me from the start that my passion was for running things, rather than for advising those who had that privilege. After a few years, I left consulting to join a tech startup, and my hours were even more grueling than they'd been at the firm. It was at that startup that I met my wife, Jane, and after we married we decided to diversify—she stayed in technology and I moved over to a large manufacturing company, running digital analytics. That led to other plum assignments and then an offer to move to Intrepid, a relatively small but well-respected retail company.

I was hired to join the strategy team and within a few years ascended to chief operations officer. Then, ultimately, the brass ring: after six years at Intrepid, just as I was entering my midforties, I was offered the CEO role.

I'd known and admired the previous CEO, the affable and gregarious Toby Manfield, since my first days at the company. He'd been in the role for more than a decade. Two years ago, Toby had a cancer scare and made no bones about the fact that he feared for his life. A timely intervention and the work of a skillful surgeon spared him, but he returned a changed man. Last year, he announced his decision. Although he was ten years from conventional retirement age, he would leave Intrepid for a leadership role in the nonprofit sector. His departure was abrupt and amicable. He and the board agreed on me as a successor, but we did not have much time to overlap and plan. The board needed a strong hand at the helm right away. Fortunately, Jane and I felt that this move lined up with the priorities for our family. I accepted with pride and pleasure.

When I joined it, Intrepid was a sixty-year-old company that had once been at the top of its category. Sure, there were press reports that it was resting on its laurels, and even my children can tell you that retail in the twenty-first century is an industry under siege (Jane and I never lost the habit of talking about work over dinner). But I was sure that I was up to the challenge. I was particularly impressed with the experience of the board. We could energize this company, I believed. By leading with innovation and making careful investments, Intrepid would return to the top.

Now here I am, six months after taking the job. When I interviewed with the board in the weeks after Toby announced his retirement, I was full of confidence—and I promised them that they'd see a real difference right away. But now, from the CEO seat, I see the company as it really is—all the angles and issues that weren't as clear from the operations perspective. There's just no way we will make our growth targets this year; we barely made them last year. And if we don't find a way to cut costs, some private equity firm will gladly do it for us: forced acquisitions haunt my dreams. I've seen and studied this situation enough to recognize the signs of danger, but I don't yet have the experience to see how to avoid what feels, at this moment, like the inevitable.

So one Tuesday, I glanced through LinkedIn and saw that Katz had posted a link to an article he'd recently written, and it hit me: he's the perfect person to talk with. I called him immediately. It turned out he knows my predecessor. He agreed to meet me, casually and outside the office, for a one-on-one. Nothing special, I insisted, just a casual conversation. But Katz realized, as soon as he saw me, that I was under more pressure than I would readily admit.

1. Why Aligning Culture Matters

SCENE: *January, lunchtime. Casimir's, a classic steakhouse restaurant in the Midwest.*

KATZ: It's great to see you in person again, Alex. And you look terrific. Challenging positions seem to agree with you. How is Toby doing? He has been a dear friend for years. And he seemed very supportive of you.

ALEX: He was. It was gratifying. And I hear that he's very satisfied with his new role leading the nonprofit and shaking things up already.

KATZ: I'm glad to hear that. And I'm glad the board picked you. How is your new job going?

ALEX: Well, you and I have known each other for a long time, so I won't put a happy face on it. Most of our people seem happy that we have a new CEO in place. Or at least that's what they tell me. But seriously, we've got a lot of problems. Intrepid has been falling behind. We haven't hit our top-line or bottom-line numbers in the last two quarters since I became CEO. This is worse than the hit we took some years ago, when Amazon first began to compete with us. We recovered then—the nature of our products means that customers like to touch and feel before they buy, so we'll always have brick-and-mortar locations. But now sales are drying up again.

Meanwhile, there's so much we need to invest in. Of course, like everybody else, we need to improve our customer experience online, so we have a digital initiative underway. It's taking a long time to come up to speed, though, and it's costing more than we expected. We still don't do the kinds of analytics that some of the other big chains are doing. We hear that new retailers from China are going to come in and underprice us. And to be frank, we've underspent on cybersecurity; I'm terrified someone will hack our credit card files because we're not really prepared for it.

Everybody loved Toby, but I've been shocked to see how many problems he swept aside or played down. We knew there were challenges out there, but we thought we were stronger overall than we really are. Some of the board members warned us all along that we had to move quicker, to be more agile, to be ready to close stores and lay people off. And now they're warning me directly. My neck is on the line if I can't make a miracle happen. I don't think I have much time to turn things around.

KATZ: How are you handling the pressure?

ALEX: Well, I'm doing okay. We've had a few victories—a couple of inventory problems that were recurrent under Toby are now under control. I altered some reporting lines, moved boxes on the org chart, and it seemed to clarify who owned the core issue, at least around that specific inventory problem. But I shouldn't have had to pay attention to details like that. And all sorts of other crises are coming across my desk that should be handled further down the line. I suspect that the top team sometimes escalates an issue to me just to avoid having tough conversations among themselves; we like to slap each other on the back and talk about what a great team we are, how we're all such great friends, but I'm questioning what the difference is between being convivial and being conflict avoidant.

KATZ: There isn't really a difference: they're two halves of the same coin. We'll get back to that in time. For now, suffice it to say, every CEO I've ever known has complained about the top team.

ALEX: [*Sighs*] I don't want to be that guy, pointing fingers. Every one of my direct reports is superqualified. They've got the right intentions and their credentials are as good as anyone's in the industry, and I know they tell the truth.

KATZ: But . . . ?

ALEX: But they don't see how much trouble we'll be in if we don't change how we do a lot of things now. And when I address it with them in one-on-ones, mostly they blame each other. So the needle isn't moving.

KATZ: How about the rest of the company? What's the culture like? How do people feel about the way things are going?

ALEX: It's pretty bad. Departments don't feel recognized. There is a lot of infighting—most departments don't like working with each other. People complain about one another, then turn around and behave in the exact same way. We need a performance culture to replace our excuse culture!

KATZ: How do you know all this?

ALEX: We've done an engagement survey for the past few years. The data shows a general erosion in people's faith in the direction of the company. Most worrisome to me is a question about how connected the respondent feels to the company's mission—the number of people who responded positively to that was very low, around 37 percent.

KATZ: I'd be concerned about that too. But I'll caution you not to rely on engagement surveys alone—they can be a pretty blunt instrument when it comes to cultural challenges. I haven't seen many leaders make good use of those sorts of scores without supplementing them with other insights.

ALEX: I'd like to hear more about that. But you also get a sense of people's mood by just walking around the halls. The other day, I stuck my head into the real estate management group and asked a manager, this guy named Michael, why he seemed so out of sorts. "No matter what I do for people here," he said, "nobody says thank you." I hate to say it, but I agree with Michael. Even worse, no one takes responsibility. When something goes awry, we point fingers and make excuses. That's what the culture's like.

KATZ: What are you doing so far to change things?

ALEX: That's why I want to talk to you. We need to light some kind of fire to wake people up. So I've been thinking about some drastic measures: closing stores, divesting some part of the business, making a bold move with a balance sheet. Just to send a message: "It's serious this time! You're holding us back!" [*Alex's voice gets a little too loud, and Katz raises an eyebrow and looks around the restaurant. They both laugh a little, as people do when they've known each other a long time; then Alex starts again in a softer tone.*] Obviously, I get that that isn't the right approach. If I started to let people go for holding the company back, I'd have to replace half the company. So we're looking at a reorg.

KATZ: Moving some boxes on the org chart again.

ALEX: Yes, but with real purpose. And not just doing it to fix one issue, really being bold. Maybe shaking things up and getting a fresh start will help.

KATZ: What was Toby's point of view on the current cultural situation and whether or not it was working in Intrepid's favor? What did he say before he left?

ALEX: Toby and the board felt strongly that the company needed to make changes around increasing efficiency and reducing waste—we had some strategy work done two or three years ago that spelled that out in no uncertain terms. A few cross-functional initiatives got started around that time, but they weren't consistently applied, so it's hard to see whether they had any effect. Right before he left, Toby sent out a sternly worded company-wide memo, spelling out our strengths, our problems with online and inventory, and the consequences for us if we didn't raise our bottom line.

KATZ: And the response?

ALEX: Mixed. Most of the people in the company tried to justify what we were doing. "The whole industry is changing; it's not our fault" or "We're not paying our people enough," or "Some other department is screwing up"—that kind of thing.

KATZ: Most people probably just want to keep doing what they're comfortable doing and hope that somebody else thinks of the brilliant idea that will save the company.

ALEX: Yeah. And it could be that playing it safe is the best option for now anyway: we're doing well enough to keep from going under this year or next. But I don't know how long that will last. [*Pauses*] So what do you think?

KATZ: Well, at least you're not starting from scratch. A lot of companies don't even have a clue about what matters most to their people. They think it's all about the money. Their leaders seldom consider how people actually feel. At least you have identified some of the emotional aspects of the problem already, even though you haven't said it in those words.

ALEX: What do you mean?

KATZ: The crux of the problem is your cultural situation. What's holding you back isn't just outside Intrepid's doors but inside its walls: the way your people feel, think, behave, and relate to one another. In other words, the way they work together. That's why everybody's so frustrated—even you. Look at the way you talked about change. Maybe a reorg. Maybe a few layoffs of redundant staff. You don't sound convinced that any decisions you make actually could inspire or catalyze real change.

ALEX: I've been there before. I want to be optimistic, but in the back of my mind I know it never works.

KATZ: No, it never does. Or rather, to be more specific, you see a few impulsive responses right away, but you rarely see the kind of sustained results that lead to true transformation. [*Pauses*] Look, you're a well-established company. Most of your people have been here a long time.

None of them are going to change easily what they do or how they do it. Bad habits persist. Culture is stubborn and self-reinforcing.

ALEX: So you're saying I can't fight culture. What does that mean? Do we just go slowly into oblivion?

KATZ: No. You have to find a way to get important emotional forces in your current culture working with you. You identify and make use of what already exists. You have not yet said much about the *positive* emotional commitment that many people already have to Intrepid. It has to be there—there is always a reason other than a paycheck that people show up for work every day. Chances are, there are some reservoirs of genuine positive emotional energy lurking somewhere within your current cultural situation that can be harnessed if brought to light.

ALEX: You mean by proclaiming some grandiose mission? Toby did that with his "green store" initiative. Everyone thought he was completely out of touch. They hated that stuff. Posters about recycling and protecting the watersheds were practically flying off the walls when Toby left.

KATZ: Well, Toby is a nice guy. Great fun on bike-a-thons. But a top-down approach like what you describe is exactly the opposite of what I mean when I talk about generating emotional commitment. Toby decided what he thought others would get excited about instead of putting a finger to the pulse of the emotional connections people have with Intrepid. I don't think you'll make the same mistake.

ALEX: I don't think it's possible to make an emotional connection with ten thousand people.

KATZ: Maybe you're not focusing on the right places or asking the right people. Have you ever really listened to your company's people down in the enterprise? Do you know what they care about, why they come to work in the morning? How they describe to their kids what they do for a living? Believe it or not, if you're ready to hear it, people really will open up to you. And you don't have to ask everyone—just the people who intuitively understand "how things get done around here." The best thing you can do, if you want to start a movement, is to empower Intrepid people to start solving their own problems—and then get out of the way.

EVERY COMPANY HAS CULTURAL CHALLENGES

Most companies are founded with high energy and lofty aspirations. They need to be. Just earning enough to pay people is a prodigious challenge for startups. They also want to delight customers, produce remarkable products and services, and make a mark on the world—and, of course, turn a healthy profit. But over time, these ideal early aspirations tend to erode. Executives and employees lower their expectations, often without realizing it. They come to believe that only a limited kind of success is practical or realistic. When times are tight, they cut budgets without necessarily considering the long-term implications. When times are good, they become complacent and fail to acknowledge and recognize the cultural forces that enable success. They overlook and even lose the value inherent in their culture.

When corporate boards fire CEOs, the official reason is often a lack of financial success or failure to meet targets. But each is an outcome of a deeper issue: an inability to connect strategic choices and operational shifts to the company's people in ways that motivate and energize them. The CEO has set goals that people aren't prepared to meet or has made promises that the enterprise can't yet deliver. And people can't perform at their best because they lack direction and operational support, as well as the emotional energy to deliver at a higher level than the status quo.

Cultures are important and powerful because they determine what your company is capable of doing. An organizational culture is a collection of deeply held attitudes, entrenched habits, repeated behaviors, latent emotions, and collective perceptions of the world. Culture is the shared set of assumptions we all bring when we work together—our unspoken expectations of one another. Do people in your company start meetings on time, or is it okay to be a few minutes late? Would eyebrows lift if someone in the room opened and ate a bag of chips, talked openly about a personal situation, or answered emails on a smartphone while listening to the conversation? Does the company have shared stories that "everybody knows," even shared jokes that wouldn't make sense to others who hadn't ever worked there? These and hundreds of other daily choices, actions, and occurrences are visible examples of behaviors that constitute the fabric of a shared culture. This amalgam builds up over time, influenced and shaped by each individual. Leaders may be in a natural position to have a greater impact, but people at all levels are a part of the fabric. People in organizations naturally influence and are influenced by those around them; their attitudes, feelings, behaviors, and perceptions come to echo one another, to have a "family resemblance." The patterns of these interactions take on a presence that is greater than the behavior of any single individual. Everything co-alesces into an informal but broad-based and well-estab-lished sense of what is appropriate and what is not: "how we do things around here."

(If you completed the paragraph above and thought, "Wait, so what is the definition of culture?" or are tempted to fold down the corner of this page to come back to later and see if you agree, let us call your attention to the glossary (see page 151), where we've tried to provide relatively lucid definitions of the abstract terms like *culture* on which our methodology is premised. We hope that this will be a useful tool and primer to you, both as you read and as you refer to this book in your future pursuits. In other words, *those* are the pages whose corner should be turned down.)

It's also true—and this sounds like a bit of a paradox, but stay with us—that every company has both an overarching, consistent culture and competing, divergent subcultures. To understand this point, it might help to step back for a min-ute and look at one of Katz's favorite images, what he likes to call the "three circles" slide (exhibit 1.1). This is an image that has, over the course of the past few decades, been drawn by Katz on more restaurant napkins, PowerPoint slides, and hotel conference room flip charts than one can possibly be-gin to count. Leaders never seem to tire of it, though, be-cause it makes an elegant point about culture.

Within a company, we all agree that business strategy is our driving direction, the grounds on which we all have decided that we are best positioned to compete. And our operating model is how we plan to get there—the way we structure our reporting relationships and governance such that it will best support the kinds of activity that will help

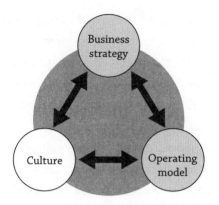

Exhibit 1.1 Coherent elements of effective organizations

us achieve that strategy. Culture is the third component: the motivation that drives and supports both other elements. It's the emotional commitment people feel (or don't feel) when the leaders describe the strategy. It's the commitment and passion that people bring to their roles, to the daily actions that will support any direction. When we say that no culture is all good or all bad or that the highest intent of leaders should not be to fix or change their culture but to align it with their strategy, this is the delicate balance that we always picture—the triad of business strategy, operating model, and culture.

The Katzenbach Center conducts a broad global survey on culture and change, with responses from more than two thousand participants. Repeating this survey allows us to track how ideas evolve over time. Year after year, the survey demonstrates that leaders at all levels view culture, strategy, and operating model as interdependent. In fact, most respondents even assert that culture is *more* important to the success of their enterprise than the other two. And significantly, each time we run this survey, the percentage of respondents who assert this increases. The fact that culture determines an enterprise's success is an idea whose time has come.

If you agree that strategy, operating model, and culture are all interdependent, then you'll likely accept the next point as well: just as no complex company has one singular strategy or operating model, no company has a single monolithic culture. Strategies shift and evolve in real time; people make decisions that mostly line up but sometimes diverge—and this can be chaotic, or sometimes it can lead to innovation. Operating models are drawn on paper, but we all know that no org chart ever really captures the complex, organic ways that working relationships thrum and churn. Every company has a cluster of strategies and operating models working in dynamic tension. Sometimes this is explicit, and sometimes it's implicit. The same is true of any company's subcultures: they exist and bounce up against each other like branches of a family tree at a reunion. Is this a problem? Not unless serious friction or misalignment exists.

Leaders of large companies are trained to recognize and address any signs of misalignment between operating model and strategy. They also tend to try to tinker with these if anything about the way that their organization is operating seems to be out of sync. (Think of Alex and how his first idea was that he could fix his culture issues through a reorganization.) The cultural forces are much more difficult to recognize and far harder to address. Therefore, even leaders who nod their heads vigorously at the "three circles" image let the topic of culture slide way down to the bottom of the agenda. But even if nobody talks or thinks about it, every company still has a strong cultural situation that needs to be cohesively aligned with the other elements.

The driving forces of any cultural situation are emotional rather than rational. This is why culture feels so unfamiliar and mysterious to most leaders. Culture doesn't respond to the same levers and pulleys as other types of organizational elements. It tends to elude the traditional change management approaches that many company leaders adopt: large, wholesale transformation efforts. These approaches can be very useful at rechanneling the formal aspects of an organization. They can help roll out communications during a merger, articulate the case for change to a large organization in trouble, or realign incentives to fit a company's strategy. But when it comes to emotional energy, traditional change management efforts can fall short. They don't catalyze the deep and lasting changes that a company typically needs most, those that depend on the authentic emotional engagement of the people involved.

If you are truly interested in having your company transform—if you genuinely want a high-performance organization with a broad cadre of people committed to the success of the enterprise—then you need to become conversant with the emotions, behaviors, and deep-seated attitudes that exist in your company. You need to know what employees feel strongly about, both positively and negatively. We call this knowledge "cultural insight"—it's the clarity that allows you to truly see what motivates your people. Then, with this knowledge fully in your grasp, you can move to what we call "cultural action," targeted interventions that influence how people behave from day to day. These actions are what can influence the whole climate of how employees behave, think, and feel, bringing it into dynamic coherence with the company's strategic aspirations. To put this simply, first you need to understand your culture; then you can work within it. This is how to bring out the best in your organization.

Fortunately, this is easier to do than it might seem. And the payoff is immense. Imagine that you are part of a company with a truly vibrant cultural situation: a place where people have paid attention, in the right way, to the attitudes, beliefs, and behaviors of others throughout the enterprise. This is a business with positive urgency—the kind of atmosphere you get when people feel a high level of emotional energy and a commitment to what they do and how they do it. Employees want to move the enterprise forward, not just because they have been given incentives to do so, but because they have a collective sense of responsibility to helping achieve the stated goals. They believe that their own daily actions contribute to these goals and that they will be recognized for their contribution. They have a strong sense of mutual accountability; they don't want to let each other down. They are rarely bored, stressed, or anxious; they demonstrate inspiration and energy in everything they do. They collaborate willingly and naturally—and feel good about doing it. When you ask if they are aware of the reasons for the organization's success, they don't just say yes—they start talking about it at length and expressing their feelings about it in different ways. And then, before long, they are talking about how they can make it better still.

Many companies have, to some extent, cultures like this. They feel very different from one another because healthy cultures are distinctive. For example, at Zappos, the online shoe store owned by Amazon, employees feel personally engaged about their relationships with customers. They apply creativity and ingenuity on the job, knowing that customers appreciate it and feeling proud of what they can do. At paradigm-shifting Airbnb, people in every role believe passionately in the company's mission of hospitality as a radical idea of feeling at home anywhere in the world and look at every aspect of their business as an opportunity to support and further that idea. At a financial-services institution we have advised in South Africa, employees feel a similarly strong sense of emotional commitment—but in this case it's to their shared mission to help Africa, "our home." The institution has a history of supporting and building the economies of the continent that has lasted for more than a century. A similar outlook exists at one of the largest energy companies in the world. Other companies with strong cultures, such as USAA (an American insurance company for military employees, veterans, and their families) and Southwest Airlines, are known for the way the company cares about customers' feelings and energizes its employees: not just the top management but all employees are encouraged to fulfill their aspirations.

Successful companies can have widely divergent cultures, even in the same industry. Consider, for example, Starbucks and Dunkin' Donuts, two retail chains that serve coffee and food. They are both known for their continued growth and their ability to satisfy customers. Starbucks built its culture around the concept of a "third place," besides home and work, and everything about it is oriented to premium conviviality. Dunkin' Donuts has a culture built around efficiency, frugality, and getting things done. Its slogan, "America runs on Dunkin'," is not just a marketing message. It reflects the culture of the chain. The business has shaped the culture, but the culture has also shaped the business.

You could make a similar comparison across Apple, Intel, Google, and Microsoft—all in the technology industry but with four very different cultures—or Aetna and Geico; FedEx, UPS, and DHL; Unilever and Procter & Gamble; Burberry and Brooks Brothers; Delta, British Airways, and Southwest Airlines; and Four Seasons Hotels and Airbnb.

Even when people agree on a high-level direction for an organization or support a strategy intellectually, they have to make a next step: asking how their *own* actions and decisions and working norms need to alter to make that strategy work. "Emotional support" enters the picture here: people's in-the-minute reactions and choices are mostly responses to emotional stimuli rather than abstract rational thinking. This is why leaders need to consider what drives people emotionally, as well as rationally, to make a difference in how work gets done. An organization chart—in other words, the formal side of how things run—is never the whole picture. Our survey results spell this out very clearly: 52 percent of respondents agree or strongly agree that in their organization, the way things get done, the real chain of command, is not consistent with how things "should" work, on paper. People will move in new directions, outside their comfort zones, only if the culture supports them in doing so. Thus the famous Peter Drucker expression, "Culture eats strategy for breakfast."

You can move a company forward only by working with and within the current manifestations of your cultural situation: guiding it, aligning key aspects as it evolves, fostering improvement, enhancing existing values, and showing its relevance. Katz and Zia Khan's 2010 book, *Leading outside the Lines*, encourages leaders to take a bilateral view of both the formal and informal sides of organizations and to consider how they support and enhance each other. The authors urge leaders to aspire to a kind of aligned leadership that is "a holistic style that moves organizations to places they couldn't otherwise go." To do this, you need to find ways to identify and then capitalize on existing positive emotional elements embedded in that culture that are overlooked or underutilized, which can then help you accomplish a state of alignment between how people behave and feel and what makes the company successful. We call this "cultural coherence." Explaining how to achieve this is the purpose of this book. It is a step-by-step guide to harnessing the critical few elements that will help align your culture—its on-paper, formal and elusive emotional, informal elements—and put it to work.

THE CONCEPT OF THE "CRITICAL FEW"

If you work in any large or well-established organization, you already know how seemingly impassable an entrenched, repeating set of behaviors can become. A full quarter of our survey respondents reported that a culture effort initiated at their organization had resulted in no visible results. It takes persistence and attention to shift those habits, just as it does for personal habits like smoking and overeating. People don't change their habits quickly or easily, even when they have excellent reasons to do so. But habits can be changed, and cultures do evolve. And this can be guided by you.

You may be a CEO, another member of the C-suite, a middle manager, or a frontline worker—whatever role you hold in your company, you have the power to evolve the culture. You don't have to accept the culture as it is. You can accentuate the best of it and use it to help your organization

overcome patterns that seem to be interrupting your progress toward your goals. The road to that end involves selective and targeted alignment, rather than dramatic repeal and
replacement.

Once you find basic cultural elements that motivate your
workforce, you can cultivate them and align them with your
goals. These elements tap the emotions that bring a culture
to life. They are broad enough to resonate across the whole
organization but focused and simple enough to encourage
real actions in people's daily lives. They fall into three basic
categories (all of which will be elucidated in later chapters, as
well as explained in brief in the glossary):

- *Traits:* A set of shared characteristics that represent
  the "family resemblance" of your entire enterprise—
  the qualities that transcend subcultures and are at the
  heart of the shared assumptions people bring to work
  and their emotional connection to what they do.

- *Keystone behaviors:* A few carefully identified things
  that some people do, day after day, that would lead
  your company to succeed if they were replicated at
  greater scale.

- *Authentic informal leaders (AILs):* A few people, or at
  least a reasonably small percentage of your company's
  people, who stand out because they have a high degree
  of "emotional intuition" or social connectedness. (AILs
  are discussed in chapters 4 and 5.)

In our experience, a sharp focus on these critical few
elements reduces complexity and begets a positive, informal, and lasting cultural impact on performance. Most importantly, this approach takes the emotional dimension of

human behavior into account and exploits the power of simplicity. It amplifies community connections because it encourages the workforce to look to peers and colleagues for insight, support, and encouragement. When people you trust and admire model and enable a few key behaviors and help others do the same (and feel good about it!), those behaviors spread quickly, and they stick.

A focused approach like this can feel counterintuitive. Most other methodologies meet complexity with comprehensive thoroughness: initiatives, ideas, frameworks, and change plans all premised on the idea that a culture can be forcibly pushed toward some set of external standards whose achievement means that the culture work is complete. We have yet to meet the leader who can describe to us how a very comprehensive approach changed the way things really worked. Complexity is distracting; comprehensiveness is wasted energy. You need crystal-clear simplicity and a small group of elements that will carry everyone forward together. You don't need a lot of targets to hit or results to generate. You need to unify your organization's people around a common, clear cultural movement, driven by a core of keystone behaviors and positive emotions.

But simplicity requires discipline. As a leader looking for ways to help those in your sphere of influence align with the company strategy, you must make many difficult choices: resonant traits, compelling behaviors, influential "authentic informal leaders."

To recognize how hard this is, consider what would happen if you had to pick, right now, a few keystone actions your company should take immediately to build a better culture. We're sure you can easily name twelve. It's much harder to boil them down to three or four; often, you'll have a good reason to include every one of the dozen. Yet if you can't narrow down the list, you'll be overwhelmed when you start to work with them, and so will everyone else in the organization. Moreover, it will be very difficult to measure any change; you won't even know which new behaviors have catalyzed new results. If you want to be effective at change or boosting performance, you can't encompass multitudes. You need to focus your attention on the critical few.

More likely than not, the single act you will best be remembered for in the course of your career is the way in which you managed to impact a cultural situation, whether you are a leader close to the front lines or a CEO. If you identify and deploy a critical few elements within the cultural situation in your work environment, you will create clarity and meaning for others. People around you will be more likely to make an emotional, not just a rational, commitment to change. They will trust and respect your choice of direction, and they will look for ways to follow it. You will elicit enthusiasm and creativity and build the kind of powerful company that people recognize for its innate value and effectiveness. And most of all, what you do with respect to your cultural challenges will be much more important than what you say. That's the essence of emotional resonance. The rest of this book will show you how to achieve it.

2. A Critical Few Traits

SCENE: *March of the same year. Alex's office.*

KATZ: You look a bit glum. What's wrong?

ALEX: I just finished conducting an exit interview with one of our best people, a young buyer named Calvin.

KATZ: That's disappointing. What did you like about him, and why is he leaving?

ALEX: Calvin's ambitious, with great business instincts. He focused on growth goals—both for his product group and for the whole retail chain. He built relationships with some new suppliers in Europe, really interesting merchandise. One of them offered him a job, and he told me yesterday that he'll move to Germany and join them. He said the pay would be a bit more, but mainly he talked about how flexible they seemed, how much autonomy and direction he would have.

KATZ: Why did he talk to you instead of his direct boss? Were there issues there?

ALEX: Not at all—he reports to the head of supply chain, Florence, and they thought the world of each other. And Trans, our head of technology, is another one of his mentors. But I wanted to talk to him as well to find out more. I have a slush fund in my budget for a special projects role, and I thought I might be able to talk him into a rotation as my direct report. But he seemed determined to go.

KATZ: What did you learn?

ALEX: That he was fed up—not with Florence or with anyone in particular, but what he called "the bureaucracy." He said there were just too many barriers to doing his job.

KATZ: Are internal operations typically a problem?

ALEX: Yes and no. From an operating model standpoint, we have best practices in place that I'll match against any other retail chain—in HR, IT, marketing, you name it. And we're always under budget. But somehow we still don't see results. On paper we are doing everything right, but just walk around and people will tell you how much is broken.

KATZ: Tell me more. What's an issue people tend to complain about?

ALEX: Well, the purchasing group always has a bone to pick about our travel policies. Like most retail companies, we aim for pretty lean operations, and this includes a policy that anyone below VP level fly economy. This is fine for domestic flights. It's tough for Europe, though, and murderous for Asia! And the purchasing team, who are all below VP, are the ones whom the policy hits hard because most of our suppliers are outside the US. Imagine that you're on that team. A few times, you probably do the right thing and fly to China to meet with vendors. But navigating those relationships on a different continent on just a few hours of sleep is really tough. We've noticed that these trips are happening less and less, and who can blame them? We save a few thousand on airfare each time that they travel, but overall the company ends up shortchanged.

KATZ: How so?

ALEX: Our product mix this season looks a little lackluster. I'm beginning to conclude that the purchasing group would have made better decisions if they had felt more supported in their efforts to go the extra mile to uncover better options. I'm frustrated because I feel like I shouldn't have to be the one to tell people when to bend a rule and why—I want them to have better judgment!

KATZ: What else are you seeing?

ALEX: It struck me the other day that our marketing group also has fallen into some ways of working that might be getting in the way of our goals. Everything they produce is perfect before it goes out the door. That's hard to complain about, right? But a ton of material is written that nobody ever sees. Or we hit a trend two months too late and everyone wonders why we missed the boat. I tried to raise this with Avery, the head of marketing, and he looked horrified. It was like I was trying to get his team to lower their standards instead of trying to work more efficiently. The ways that people work, the things that they congratulate themselves on having achieved—a perfect, flawless document—are at odds with how I believe we need to operate to beat our competitors.

KATZ: That's a great example. It's not that, per se, perfectionism is a bad quality. There are situations when striving for perfectionism can save everybody from costly mistakes. But there are also situations where the perfectionist habits slow things down, keep people feeling bogged down and frustrated, like they can't accomplish what they are being asked to do—a feeling we describe, in my line of work, as one of the symptoms of "cultural incoherence." But don't worry—the lecture isn't starting yet. Go on. What else is on your mind?

ALEX: There's the problem of waste. We have as many problems with environmental compliance as any company with brick-and-mortar locations. But we could cut significant cost and materials, and save money in the bargain, if we had a more comprehensive waste-reduction program. One-off ideas pop up—like installing motion-sensor lights in break rooms, having drivers turn off trucks instead of letting them idle to save on fuel costs—but nothing ever seems to stick or gain momentum. We never take ideas far enough to see real results.

KATZ: Do the functional leaders talk to each other about these problems?

ALEX: Not much. They are all at different places. For example, in people practices, some of our leaders are really good at motivating their groups. Others beat down their people and push hard with threats. We don't have any discussion about which approach works best for us—or even when each approach is most appropriate. My gut tells me that the former is more effective than the latter—after all, it was you who taught me that pride matters more than money, and certainly more than stern lectures. [*At this, Katz smiles.*] But I don't have any data to back that up. Before I confront the leaders who have the reputation of being really hard drivers, I want data to make my case. Until I get that, it's a lot of rumors and anecdotes without any real specific examples of what works and why.

KATZ: Have you talked to different functional leaders about, well, inviting each other to meetings and confronting these problems more openly and directly?

ALEX: I've made some strong suggestions, and my heads look at me like, "You've got to be kidding!" I feel like I need to be really specific; if I try to just say, "Hey, everybody, start working together," I'm sure that I'll be ignored. For example, marketing and IT need to jointly develop a customer analytics system; we're capturing the data at the stores and online, but as yet we have no real system that lets us pull out any useful insights. But both sides have been holding back on saying what they can offer. They seem more concerned with protecting their turf than making a new idea happen. Meanwhile, the finance department can send in a budget, and then accounts payable won't sign off on it. Weeks of work by the finance team squandered, decisions stalled. It's ridiculous. But truly, I can't step into every decision and interaction.

KATZ: And let me guess. Your leaders say that they can't behave differently because of obstacles and attitudes embedded in the system. Secretly meaning there's no reward, it doesn't help them move up the ladder, or others will get in the way. Basically, it is just not worth the time.

ALEX: Yeah. And there are some real bureaucratic obstacles, such as having to get permission to even talk to someone else's supplier. Some of this has to do with rivalries, fiefdoms, fights over turf. People believe that they're all vying for the same funds, even when that isn't true, even when they pull from separate parts of the overall budget.

At times I suspect there's some backstory no one will tell me, happening years before I came on the scene, that has led to alliances and grudges I'll never understand. But I refuse to believe that unearthing old stories will fix what's broken. I'm ready to just yell out, "Everybody get over it!"

KATZ: And the biggest factor in your favor is that most everyone cares about the company in one way or another—right?

ALEX: Yes, they absolutely care about the company. They just aren't sure how they feel about each other.

KATZ: [*Laughs*] Well, I have some good news for you.

ALEX: I could use some.

KATZ: Last time we met, I said that I didn't think your company was too bad off compared to others I've seen. I still believe that. Even the complaints and fights can give you some reason to be hopeful. Frustration is on the opposite end of the spectrum from apathy, which is the most dangerous condition in any organization. Frustration suggests that people want to see change; they're aware that there are problems. They're blaming each other—or "the system" in general—because they don't see a clear path forward. And since their emotions are involved, you can't just tell them what to do. You have to make them see and actually anticipate feeling good about taking advantage of their common interest.

ALEX: I'll get right on it. I'll have a memo out to them tomorrow.

KATZ: [*Laughs*] What are you really doing about it?

ALEX: Well, I already sat down with our head of HR, Elin. She's a fixture here; she started her career under Martin, the CEO who preceded Toby. She told me about a "values" exercise that the organization went through seven or eight years ago. That wasn't too long before I began working here, but I told her I've never heard anyone mention the values in my conversations with people across the company, including the former CEO! Elin wants to revisit and refresh the values for a new era, but I'm skeptical about what that would accomplish.

KATZ: Values—what an organization stands for—absolutely have a part in this discussion, but I agree with your instinct that the conversation about culture can't begin and end there. However, let's back up a little. Tell me more about these conversations you've been having with people.

[*At this, Alex brightens.*]

ALEX: The last conversation I had with you, in January, really encouraged me to continue, and even expand, the efforts I've been making to have one-on-one or informal small group conversations. Not just with department heads but employees all across the company. I asked my assistant to expand every scheduled distribution site visit from a half day to a full day and kept the second half of the day clear so I could just wander around and talk to people one-on-one. I also make every effort to take hierarchy and authority out of the room during these discussions, although I know that is hard to do. Make sure everybody calls me by my first name—that's always a good start.

KATZ: [*Nods approvingly*] What are you hearing?

ALEX: When we last met, you pushed me to understand Intrepid on its own terms. So I've been asking people to describe the company: "What is it about us that makes us special?" "What does Intrepid mean to you?" But I have to confess, I didn't get very far. People seemed a little flummoxed by the questions—one person even took out our marketing materials and talked me through our tagline and mission statement, as if I'd never seen them before!

[*They both laugh.*]

KATZ: That was a terrific start. And I'm also not surprised to hear that you spun in circles a little, and I'm glad we're meeting again.

To develop an accurate sense of your culture, the set of habits and behaviors and beliefs that determine how work gets done, you have to be a little indirect. Most of the time, as you just experienced, people seem to get overwhelmed by the culture topic—it feels too unwieldy to put into words. Instead it helps to keep conversations focused on behaviors—real, observable, tangible behaviors, things that people do every day in the course of going about the daily business of their work. And then you will stay alert to when these behaviors elicit some kind of emotional response, negative as well as positive. That emotional response tells you that those behaviors are touching on, catalyzing, generating—or getting in the way of—a sense of connectedness between people.

And you don't just ask the top few layers—or even necessarily start at the top, although you do want to keep the top team involved. You go through the company, and you pull together some discussion groups at different levels. You ask about strengths and weaknesses and start to build a picture. For instance, you might ask, "What do you tell neighbors at a weekend barbecue about why you like working at Intrepid?" "What does your best day look like?" "When are you excited to go to work?" "What do you tell your spouse when you don't want to go to work?" "What keeps you up with worry at night?" From these conversations, and from other data points that turn up along the way—the "official" ones, like employee surveys and the values statements you mentioned, as well as "unofficial" ones, like shared jokes that everybody seems to know—you start to build a much more realistic picture of Intrepid's culture challenges and opportunities. It's just like developing your business strategy. The final product should be simple: a list of core traits that are accessible to all, a language that everyone can understand. But it takes a lot of input and iterations to get it right.

ALEX: What's an example of a trait? Would it be something like integrity?

KATZ: No, I wouldn't call integrity a trait. Integrity is a value—something we aspire to. If I believe that I work in an organization that has integrity, that belief gives meaning and purpose to my work. It strengthens my emotional connection to the others around me. Values, when well articulated and demonstrated, do this very well—they give us something to aspire to. But it's hard to connect a conversation about values to the real work that people do every day, except in very ideal terms. And values don't make much of a difference in performance until they are reflected in what highly respected people do as a result.

ALEX: [Looking thoughtful] Or unless a value seems to be missing. I had to fire someone for stepping out of line last year, related to integrity.

KATZ: I'm sorry to hear that—but that's correct. And it underscores what I'm saying. Values are necessary and are also aspirational. Like strategy, they are always out ahead of us—they are what we are trying to achieve. Establishing values, and using them as touchstones to remind us all how to be our best selves, is a crucial part of any effort to work on culture. But values alone don't define a culture. Values reflect how you want things to be done; traits reflect how things are done today.

ALEX: So if integrity is a value, tell me about a trait. What's a trait you see at Intrepid?

KATZ: I'll use your own words. You've described the company to me as thrifty and very process focused: these are perfect examples of traits. A trait is a tendency to work in a certain way. It ties directly to performance. And crucially, it's neutral—you can see how sometimes it helps the business and sometimes it gets in the way. We've all worked with someone who followed every process to the letter and still wasn't deemed high potential and put on the fast track to manager. Being process driven has both strengths and weaknesses. And when you get people to talk about that, you can start to have conversations about culture that feel like they might lead to real change.

ALEX: It's interesting that you mention both strengths and weaknesses. Why weaknesses? You seem to encourage that I take a very positive view of Intrepid's culture. Wouldn't you, then, encourage me just to focus on its strengths?

KATZ: Strengths and weaknesses are two sides of the same coin. If you can't recognize the weak side of a trait, its potential downside, then you aren't looking at the whole picture. Most importantly, you miss the full set of emotions people have around a trait—the sense of accomplishment and pride that people in a thrifty organization feel when they stay within budget and find clever ways to save resources, as well as the exasperation and annoyance that they feel when they sense that others are shortchanging them, being penny-wise and pound-foolish. Traits are both sources of energy and potential obstacles to what you need to do to succeed. You have to name and recognize them to be able to deal with them in all their complexity.

ALEX: Can I change the company's traits?

KATZ: It's so much easier to work with what you have than to try to change the fundamental nature of your organization. Let's stay with thrift as an example. In an industry with margins as tight as yours, you'd be a fool to try to get rid of it, right? What you need to do is acknowledge it, reward it where it helps you, and point out where it gets in the way.

ALEX: Are you saying that I can't change Intrepid?

KATZ: No, that isn't what I'm saying. But here's the bad news: major change will be slower than you want it to be—it can take decades versus months or years. That's why I refer to it as "evolution." But if you commit and are consistent, evolution also can be real and lasting. That's the secret that the best leaders know, and that's what I'd like to help you accomplish.

ALEX: It's frustrating to hear that change is slow. But at the same time, I've never heard anyone tell the story of an organization or institution that changed overnight. I believe what I'm hearing. Let's try it your way. Given the complexity, where do you suggest we start?

KATZ: When's your next leadership team meeting?

ALEX: Mid-May.

KATZ: Great, that gives us some time to be purposeful about how you engage them. I think that the values exercise that Elin suggested is a good idea. If Elin brought it up, she is surely seeking a way to help you align key emotional elements of your cultural situation, and that's the tool she's familiar with. So let's make that the window we move through. It's a good enough place to begin.

Then, that leadership team meeting can be a chance to engage the other executives on the topic of culture more broadly. In the interim, why don't you name Elin and a few others to help you, and together you can run some interviews of the type that I described. Give Florence a call—if she sees the link between Intrepid's culture and the loss of one of her best people, Calvin, she'll be motivated to work with us to try to see what's going on.

From those interviews, we can develop at least a rough draft version of what Intrepid's traits might be. A conversation about values, what you aspire to, is an excellent time to also talk about who you are as a company, how you work every day.

ALEX: Florence is just down the hall—I'll go talk to her now. And I like your use of "we." I suppose this means you're offering to help?

KATZ: [*Smiles*] Well, I can't think of anything I'd rather do.

WHAT ARE TRAITS, AND WHY ARE THEY IMPORTANT TO CULTURE?

Traits are at the heart of any organization. They are the essential characteristics that form the scaffolding for how any group of people thinks, feels, and behaves. They are the stable, prominent qualities that are shared across a company. For any leader who seeks to understand a business's cultural challenges and how it operates, it's important to start by surfacing and articulating these critical few traits. The process of doing so—the diagnosis, the self-reflection, and the narrowing down—is a crucial first step to both evolving and aligning an organization's cultural influence on how people behave to get things done emotionally as well as rationally in any organization—the cultural insight step described in chapter 1.

Why do the traits matter? Let's start with an analogy—in fact, let's start by considering Alex himself, who is (we hope) becoming clearer to you as a person over the course of this story. Alex has values that he holds dear, like taking care of the people he works with and behaving with integrity. These values have resonance for him and are ideals he aspires to consistently meet, ways that he likes to think about himself, his colleagues, and his goals. Alex also has a core set of personality traits, such as self-confidence and ambition. These are so essential to Alex that they might not even be clear to him—they are like the bones beneath his skin, the fundamental matter of which Alex is made. If you wanted Alex to change or evolve in some way—let's say that, for the good of his company, you wanted Alex to have more conversations with his leadership team and spend less time scrutinizing numbers that could just as ably be overseen by his CFO—you would be wise to understand and build from not just the values Alex aspires to but also several of the key personality, character, and gender traits that now govern how he acts day to day. Any efforts to understand, work with, and even evolve Alex as a person must begin with an understanding of these traits and an acceptance that they'll be slow to change.

Are we implying that people (and, by analogy, organizations or organizational culture) can't be changed? Let's emphasize the answer here—this is a crucial point at the heart of this methodology. *Organizations can change (or, rather, evolve)—but only if that change is grounded in a solid sense of the steady state of that organization.* It is well documented that most organization-wide attempts at changing culture fall short of the original intent; as we noted in chapter 1, one quarter of the Katzenbach Center survey respondents reported that an effort had been made to change their company's culture and that they had seen no difference whatsoever as a result. This "failure to budge" on the part of culture is due to leaders' skipping the "traits" step—that is, refusing to surface, articulate, and commit to working with their organization's core differentiating qualities. It is a result of jumping to solutions without pausing for self-reflection and diagnosis.

A client once told Gretchen a story of how he had interviewed at a moribund retail giant, a well-known organization whose brand reputation and profitability had been on a slow decline for decades. The client, Jeff, was interviewed by the newly minted CEO for a role on the turnaround-focused leadership team. According to Jeff, the CEO explained his strategy this way: within a year, he expected to redefine this large, slow-moving, steady-ship retailer as a technology innovation company. Jeff hightailed it out the door rather than waiting for an offer. He was wise to do so. (And the fact that he told Gretchen this story as a laugh line made it clear to her, right away, that they would work well together.)

A quick change toward what's trendy isn't wise or even possible. Leaders must begin with a solid understanding of where they are today, what "family resemblance" exists across the company. Then and only then is it possible to focus on behaviors that bring out the best, most useful aspects of these core qualities—and to encourage more of them, every day.

Recall one of Alex's core traits: ambition. Unlike his value of integrity, which is inarguably positive and aspirational, ambition is neutral. You can imagine scenarios in which Alex's ambition is useful to him as an individual and to the organization he leads. You can also picture certain days or certain situations in which this same quality causes those around Alex to roll their eyes in exasperation. Now imagine that you were Alex's executive coach. You would likely point out that he can't change the central fact of his own ambitiousness— but he can recognize and repeat the best behaviors through which it manifests, like encouraging others to set high goals. You could also teach him to notice and curb ambition-related behaviors that are less productive, like demonstrating impatience with others who are slower learners.

Similarly, in our work with organizations on culture, we strive to help people see their organization's essential traits as neutral—which does not mean that they are bland and nondescript. A trait's neutrality means that it has positive and negative repercussions. Traits also have an emotional component. When we work with organizations to deduce and define their core traits, this process always involves working through strong feelings that people have about the institution that they are part of, about how it supports them and when it feels like it stands in their way. Getting to a neutral, clear-eyed diagnostic means working through a lot of emotional nuance. Then, when the traits are presented back to the organization, another kind of emotional response occurs: the satisfying sense of recognition of commonality and the pleasure of being seen and understood.

Arriving at Your Traits

You won't be able to arrive at an accurate, emotionally resonant group of traits by asking only a few people. You'll want to engage groups of people at different levels across the organization in structured interviews and focus groups designed to surface their feelings about your organization's culture. There are many ways to approach these interactions; in the appendix, you'll find a sample focus group agenda and sample interview questions to spur your thinking.

Exhibit 2.1 lists twelve common traits from the many we've collected through our decades of research and client work. Don't be constrained by this list, however—it's provided just to give you ideas. A trait that describes ways of working at your organization may be one that is unique to your company. For example, we conducted a client diagnostic at an organization in which people loved to tell stories about the company's origin; "respect for folklore" ended up as one of its core traits. Although one could imagine how respect for folklore could get in the way of some strategic aspirations, such as innovation, it also had very deep emotional resonance for people at all levels—and we'll be surprised if it appears on a list of traits at any of our other clients.

• Consensus driven	• Cautious
• Caring	• "Above and beyond"
• Hierarchical	• Process focused
• Individualistic	• Opportunistic
• Relationship focused	• Optimistic
• Paternalistic	• Egalitarian

Exhibit 2.1 Examples of traits from our work

At a high level in the organization, the best approach to surfacing good data is to avoid direct questions, such as, "What traits are important in our culture?" As with Alex's first effort with his own employees, that kind of direct approach is likely to yield only platitudes. Instead, get people to tell stories about what's important to them. Ask what they love about coming to work, what they are proud of regarding the way that they work together, decide, and motivate. Stage some of these conversations as one-on-one interviews and others as small, informal peer groupings. You'll be surprised and delighted to hear what emerges from eight or ten people who are encouraged to share their thoughts in an appropriate, safe environment. Exhibit 2.2 is a sample of questions we have used at client engagements to spur this type of dialogue.

Also ask people what frustrates them at work. Individuals may take this opportunity to vent. Allow this, but direct the conversation away from common day-to-day complaints that are applicable to any corporate environment and focus on qualities and patterns of behavior that are unique to the

	Questions
General	What are the strengths in your culture—what makes you most proud to work here?
	What elements of your culture (e.g., the way things really get done at your company) get in the way?
Decision-Making	Who makes decisions? Do decisions tend to be made by one person or via consensus?
	Do people here tend to rely more on data and analytics in decision-making or intuition and experience?
Motivators	How important are external customers relative to internal operations?
	Is this a place where people tend to come and stay for life, or is attrition common and expected?
	Do people here tend to be more interested in history or what the future holds?
Attitudes	Is your company made up of experts or generalists?
	How tolerant of risk are people in this company?
	What is more important—self-sufficiency or collaboration?
Process and Structure	How hierarchical is your company? Are all voices treated equally, or do people defer to leaders?
	How rigid are processes? Is improvisation allowed and encouraged?

Exhibit 2.2 Sample questions

organization. If guided in this direction, individuals usually realize that many of the things that frustrate them are the flip side of the things they are proud of. You may hear something like, "We really care about our people, and sometimes that means we make the 'caring' decision rather than the 'right' decision."

Even if the folks you speak with don't make that explicit connection, you will often find that the challenges and frustrations they describe stem from sources of pride. For example, individuals working at organizations that prize individual empowerment and autonomy often express exasperation at how hard it is to get anything done that requires coordination or standardization. A common complaint is "Everybody thinks all the people here are special and wants to be granted an exemption from the rules." On the other hand, people working at highly collaborative, consensus-based organizations can be proud of having a voice in every decision that impacts them but also frustrated by the amount of time it takes to get everyone to agree.

Inevitably, subculture traits will appear. This is natural and logical. For example, traits will emerge that are more prevalent in HR and less prevalent in the finance team, like "people focused." Traits like "safety conscious" will emerge in focus groups with employees on the shop floor but never in marketing. And subcultures aren't limited to functions. Throughout the decades that we have worked in this field, we have seen an increasing trend toward globalization of large multinational organizations. Most of the companies we work with now have subcultures that cross real boundaries; potential frictions are enhanced by acute differences in language, style of dress, and even religious faith and alphabet. But do not let the presence of strong, differentiated subcultures distract you from the task of surfacing and identifying overarching traits. Our clients have included global organizations with regional offices that spanned continents and behemoth companies cobbled together by ambitious acquisitions. In every situation, a patient and thorough diagnostic has surfaced traits that were, to the surprise and agreement of all, common and consistent across the full span of the organization.

In addition to interviews and focus groups, other methods and data points can help you enrich your understanding of your culture. The Katzenbach Center team deploys a survey tool that highlights the relative prominence of traits that tend to recur across organizations, but this specific tool is not the only way to crack this nut. Many organizations conduct internal employee engagement surveys. Within our own firm, PwC, the Saratoga Institute developed one of the first consistent sets of HR metrics forty years ago and now has a cross-sector, global database through which organizations can explore how their people-related data compares to that of thousands of other companies across the globe. Whether an organization has an internal, homegrown survey that has been conducted just a few times or has a large annual survey with rigorous external benchmarking that has been done for many years, a common complaint we hear from clients is that survey results do not lead to change. But we encourage them, as we encourage you here, to take out the results and dust them off. It's all good data and can help yield the types of insights you need. Brainstorm with your trusted advisors and with thought-provoking outsiders—one company we work with actually used data from exit interviews with employees who had decided to leave, and this helped leaders pinpoint, discuss, and finally address a culture trait of bureaucracy that had bedeviled them for decades.

Whatever method you use to gather insights about your company's traits, compare the results with your own observations. Watch people in meetings, in casual conversations, and in their daily operations. Consider the surroundings as an outsider would see them: What do people display on their desks? Are the plants being watered? What are the artifacts on the walls? Observe whether people move quickly or slowly to make decisions and consider what either accelerates or impedes this process. Ask yourself whether meetings are more effusive or matter-of-fact and if that is a common preference throughout the company. Is your company naturally global in outlook, mixing people from different nationalities and backgrounds, or does it tend to remain active within just one territory or region? Does the leadership team always meet at headquarters, or do they travel to other regions? What do your people care about? What motivates them? What do they do in the workplace that they wouldn't elsewhere?

Here are some examples of observable detail from many decades of walking onto corporate campuses and beginning to discern a story about culture. Twenty-five years ago, Apple chose to name the main U-shaped drive of its headquarters campus Infinite Loop, a coding term. This playful approach was very unusual at the time, signifying a lack of propriety. Decades later, though, an irreverent (and even indulgent) approach to office space, including whimsical details like slides and scooters and perks such as free snacks and dry cleaning, has become almost an industry norm in the technology sector.

Danaher's unprepossessing offices, in the heart of Washington, DC, say that the company, while plugged into a vibrant capital city and its businesses, is resolutely unpretentious and pragmatic. A cafeteria full of lush, fresh produce and vegetarian options at a pharmaceutical company we worked with signaled a broad commitment to health and wellness. Bare-bones supply closets at a midstream energy company in Houston that had just acquired a much more extravagant (and less profitable) competitor demonstrated the core trait of extreme efficiency and thrift. At this last company, one of our consultants asked to borrow a gum eraser from an administrative assistant. The admin smiled graciously, took a large pair of scissors and a worn-down eraser out of her desk drawer, sliced that eraser in half, and handed the consultant the larger slice. It's hard to find a better example of how a real-time behavior manifests a core trait!

The goal of this detective work is to generate a list of culture traits that is unique to the organization and to understand the positives and negatives associated with these traits. You can think of a company's traits as a list of neutral descriptors, with positive manifestations (or sources of strength) on one side and negative manifestations (or challenges and barriers) on the other. For example, you may have a company that is consensus driven, in which the entire team feels ownership of decisions. This may be a valuable trait for your company because it can ensure that once a decision has been made, many people will come on board to help execute it. On the flip side, if decisions can't be made without consensus, it's very hard for an organization to act. Further, ideas can be watered down to the lowest common denominator, the least offensive one, because conflicting points of view are too threatening. Articulate all of this. The more specific you can be about the real behaviors related to a trait, the better it will be for developing an accurate picture of how this trait manifests at your company.

After you develop a "long list" of traits, select three to five key traits that best articulate your company's current cultural situation. Choose carefully, because the traits will be a touchstone in the process of evolving your culture. Traits describe, with emotional resonance, "who we are" on our best days and on our worst. To be most useful, these traits need to meet several criteria, as shown in exhibit 2.3.

Traits should

- *Reflect your company's essential nature.* People throughout the company should be able to recognize the traits as meaningful; there should be broad agreement that they articulate some core essence of how people work together.
- *Resonate across the enterprise.* These traits are not just for the engineers, the people in your home country, or the people at the top of the hierarchy. They should feel relevant to most people, even though the behavioral manifestations of one or more traits may differ across subcultures, functions, or geographics.
- *Trigger a positive emotional response.* The positives associated with the traits should be things that get people excited and that all agree will lead to a better, more effective business. Make sure the traits trigger enthusiasm for and commitment to the company's goals and that they can keep motivating your people over time.
- *Support your company's cause.* You began this culture effort for the sake of moving your company in a new direction: to be more resilient, to face an external threat, or to move toward an opportunity. The traits you select should have implications that are relevant for the direction you are trying to go in. The strengths should be sources of emotional energy that support your business goals, while the challenges are typically barriers that are holding you back.

Exhibit 2.3 Selection criteria for critical traits

Exhibit 2.4 is a sample "traits analysis" that we created, over the course of writing this book, for our fictional company, Intrepid. In the next chapter's episode of the Alex and Katz story (spoiler alert!), our estimable (and imaginary) Intrepid culture team will choose three core traits for their company: perfectionist, consensus driven, and thrifty. As part of the exercise of writing the fictionalized Intrepid case study, we pulled together a team of our practitioners, and we all brainstormed behaviors that would manifest the positive and negative sides of these traits, just as we do with our clients. Usually, this kind of analysis takes weeks of conversations, but for our purposes, we just did it over lunch. (People who work with us tend to call this kind of activity "fun"— lucky for us!) When we do this analysis with clients, we call it a "culture thumbprint." The example in exhibit 2.4 is the result of that lunchtime brainstorm. It is a good proxy for one of our clients' analyses (which are usually too intimate to be shared outside the company).

From Traits to Emotional Commitment

Emotional, irrational, messy human responses—their attachments, triggers, affiliations, identifications, resistance— are at the heart of any discussion on culture. Katz's 2003 book, *Why Pride Matters More Than Money*, posits that the best leaders and organizations in the world have succeeded due to their ability to cultivate pride in people. Katz argues that "leaders at any level who develop the capability to instill pride in others can use that ability to achieve higher levels of business performance." This was premised on the two-factor theory of job satisfaction of American psychologist Frederick Herzberg, who coined the term *motivational*

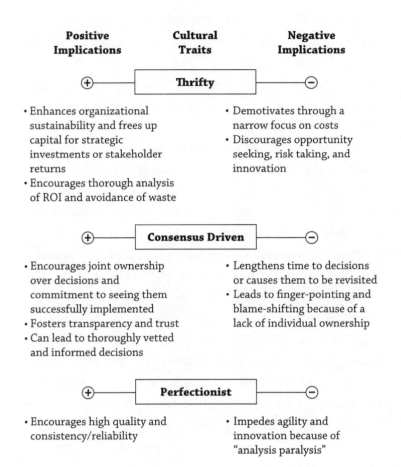

Positive Implications	Cultural Traits	Negative Implications
⊕	**Thrifty**	⊖
• Enhances organizational sustainability and frees up capital for strategic investments or stakeholder returns • Encourages thorough analysis of ROI and avoidance of waste		• Demotivates through a narrow focus on costs • Discourages opportunity seeking, risk taking, and innovation
⊕	**Consensus Driven**	⊖
• Encourages joint ownership over decisions and commitment to seeing them successfully implemented • Fosters transparency and trust • Can lead to thoroughly vetted and informed decisions		• Lengthens time to decisions or causes them to be revisited • Leads to finger-pointing and blame-shifting because of a lack of individual ownership
⊕	**Perfectionist**	⊖
• Encourages high quality and consistency/reliability		• Impedes agility and innovation because of "analysis paralysis"

Exhibit 2.4 Intrepid's culture thumbprint

factors for intangible forces that encourage good performance. One of Herzberg's notable conclusions, surprising at the time but now accepted as truth (and argued by current notables such as Daniel Pink), is the idea that work itself can serve as a motivator. In 1968, Herzberg published an article, now a *Harvard Business Review* all-time classic, titled

"One More Time: How Do You Motivate Employees?" The answer to his question is Herzberg's core message, which he repeated many times throughout his life: you motivate employees *through the work itself!* This is a fundamental belief of Katz's as well, and it's consistent with how we now approach cultural alignment organization-wide. To motivate either an individual *or* an organization, you must closely observe what is happening well and encourage more of it. Emotional commitment flourishes when it is nurtured from seeds within, not applied according to some frame or set of standards that are external to the company.

In the decade and a half since writing *Why Pride Matters*, Katz has continued to believe in its central premise, but he is also more interested in a broader range of emotions. Simultaneously, through the Katzenbach Center's research and client work, we have developed a method and structure to the process by which leaders can draw a bright line for people between how they *feel* about their work and how their work supports their organization's overall strategy and goals. And surfacing and defining an organization's traits is a necessary step to releasing those powerful emotions, to drawing that line.

But wait, you might say—so much of this chapter has been devoted to the idea of traits as *neutral*. Can traits be both neutral and emotionally resonant at once? After all, how possible is it to get misty-eyed about a term like *performance driven*? Nevertheless, time and again, we witness organizations as they move through the journey of a culture diagnostic and arrive at their traits—and we learn each time that this is truly a process of trying to apply precision and discipline to, paradoxically, open up a space for that which is *imprecise* and *undisciplined*—the emotional aspect, the nonrational, noncompliance-oriented aspects of the culture. Why is this?

Emotional energy is released as traits (and behaviors, the topic of the next chapter) are defined because traits, when well-articulated, reinforce and remind people within an organization of their sense of belonging to something larger than themselves. At the beginning of a culture diagnostic, leaders of a client organization often express skepticism that they will be able to uncover *any* common traits—they believe that their organization, unlike any other, is composed of subcultures so strong and unique that they have nothing in common but the font on their business cards and the name of the company on the letterhead. And then time and again, as we listen, assess, evaluate, and discuss, we are able to come up with some strong, resonant traits. And the members of the subcultures who had understood themselves as being so divided are able to nod their heads and say yes, we agree, that is just how we *are*. They are also able to recognize, in both the traits and behaviors, their own language that they use to describe themselves.

In recent years, we conducted a culture diagnostic for a North America–based energy company and arrived at the following four traits: consensus seeking, loyal to the company, relationship driven, and respectful of expertise. Can you guess which one catalyzed the most friction in the process of getting to agreement? It was the driest, least "relationship" focused: respectful of expertise. Within this organization, this quality was so dyed-in-the-wool and valued, it was difficult to hypothesize about its neutrality. In other words, leaders were so convinced that their experts were always right, they almost couldn't stand any conversation implying that they could be wrong!

Over the course of a few hours of good dialogue, however—supported by great, real examples that we'd surfaced through the diagnostic, like the story of a functional leader who'd reduced a subordinate to tears for posing a question that challenged her technical opinion—we were able to help the whole leadership team agree that certain habits and behaviors associated with "respectful of expertise" were indeed getting in the way of the business agenda. Here is what we repeated, over and over, throughout that conversation with the team: We were not trying to get rid of the cultural tendency to value experts—we couldn't root it out even if we tried! We were simply trying to help raise an awareness of it as a trait so that leaders could, going forward, have real conversations about when and how it got in the way.

And sometimes, a relatively neutral-sounding trait has emotional resonance that an individual applies again and again over the course of his or her career. Kate Dugan, one of our Katzenbach Center core team members, began her career at Strategy& in the days when it was Booz & Company. Firm members at the former Booz & Company shared a very hard-work ethos; even partners at the highest level did not hesitate to dig into numbers and format PowerPoint documents side by side with more junior team members. A well-defined, popularly acknowledged trait of this firm was "sleeves rolled up." It was a phrase that connoted, for members of the firm, both an approach and a set of observable, real behaviors, like staying up late, tackling hard problems, and taking pleasure in real hands-on work. As a new consultant, Kate liked this phrase very much; she thought it represented one of the best qualities of the firm and how people behaved together as a team at their finest moments. As Kate described it, the way that she learned to do real work was influenced and inspired by that phrase. Even more significantly, she mentioned that a partner had once persuaded her to do something she was afraid of, facilitating a senior meeting on her own, by using that phrase. It had emotional resonance that helped her connect a new, slightly intimidating behavior to a quality that she liked to believe that she shared.

Every great company culture is based, in part, on intrinsic attraction and emotional commitment to important aspects of the company. People want to feel rewarded and recognized. They want to feel the pleasure of being part of a team. They want to learn. They want to work with others who are capable and committed. They want to be part of a culture that fosters all these qualities. When they find such a culture, they choose to be part of the enterprise. Work is no longer just transactional. They are reminded of the passion and curiosity that led them to their chosen field. They feel they can excel at their job, and they are ready to experience feelings of pride, belonging, adventure, achievement, and other personal benefits of accomplishment.

3. A Critical Few Behaviors

ALEX: I thought they'd never leave! [*Katz and Alex laugh.*] But seriously, I've never extended the leadership team meeting from lunch until close of day before . . . people were pretty heated.

KATZ: The topic of culture can be a lively one, that's for sure. Once you get people talking, it's hard to know how to get them to stop.

ALEX: It was pretty quiet for the first fifteen minutes or so, when I introduced why we were here and talked about how I've decided that our business issues are related to culture and that we need to understand our culture better to move forward. I thought I'd lost them then.

KATZ: People are accustomed to leaders paying lip service to the topic of culture and launching a high-level "culture change" imperative—then moving on to the next thing. They've learned to tune out.

ALEX: [*Ruminatively*] Florence really saved me, though, when she brought up Calvin's departure right away and framed it as a culture issue. What was it that she said?

KATZ: [*Flips through his notebook*] Here, I wrote it down. "If we don't understand why our top people can't see a future for themselves at Intrepid, then we're not looking at our current culture and asking the right questions." [*Looks up at Alex*] Yes, that was clearly a turning point. How did you view what happened next?

ALEX: It definitely brought the issues to life for some of the team. Like the head of operations, Ross—he usually doesn't have any patience for the "fuzzy stuff" kinds of discussions. But he'd hired Calvin and he felt invested in his career, so Florence's comment made it clear to him what's at stake.

KATZ: Everything gets clearer when you surface the emotional subtext. All too often people in these discussions don't recognize the importance of acknowledging the real emotions that lie at the heart of any conversation about an incident that leaves people confused or disenchanted. The discussion helped Ross connect his emotional response to Calvin leaving—disappointment—with the larger issues of the business. That's a great start. But what do you think is at stake? What do you think the leadership team walked out of here understanding?

ALEX: I think they understand that we can't rest on our laurels—that we've been complacent for too long and that we need to modernize and move ahead or risk the end of Intrepid. That things like dragging our feet about customer analytics or procrastinating about taking cybersecurity seriously—they aren't just unrelated issues but part of a larger situation that really could endanger our long-term position.

KATZ: That's well put. You've put your finger on what we call your "cultural priority." That will anchor the discussions going forward, so it's helpful. Does it feel like a different place than how you ended your last quarterly meeting?

ALEX: It absolutely does—it felt like there was a lot less finger-pointing. Avery is still cynical, but Avery will always be the cynic. However, even his habit of poking holes in arguments felt more constructive today.

KATZ: I agree. It's clear that Travis and Florence did a good job engaging a lot of stakeholders, including most of these leaders, while they developed the list of traits. Most of the people in the room felt like they'd had a hand in the process, so they felt invested in the outcome. And I liked that you'd gotten feedback from middle management and even some frontline people as well. Are you happy with where the traits landed? Do any of them surprise you? Do they feel like they represent Intrepid?

ALEX: I completely agree with "thrifty." [*Smiles*] The skeptics might even call us "cheap." You nailed that one right away in our last conversation, so I was pleased how often it came up in the interviews over the past few weeks and in the room today. And "consensus driven": that's us to a tee. We can't make a decision without talking to twenty other people, and we end up moving toward the least offensive rather than the boldest course of action. "Perfectionist" I found harder to get my head around. I've always thought people here were obsessed with processes and such rule followers. It's interesting to me to see it as perfectionism, but of course that might be because it's the trait I identify with the least. I don't care if things are perfect—I just want them to get done! [*They both laugh.*]

KATZ: As much as you like to get things done, I don't think it's yet time to declare victory. It's not enough to have a compelling "future state"—you need to motivate people to take real steps toward that aspiration. You've developed a real, collective, dare I say "consensus driven" [*winks*] point of view about Intrepid's culture today. These traits underlie how you all operate. This is the first step in aligning culture behind strategy. And you have made a good start on the second step, which is understanding how these traits are making people feel.

You've also articulated more clearly where you'd like to get to—a more modern organization, one that can move quickly with bold ideas, better execution, and more practical ways of approaching costs. The next step is behaviors. You want to show how people can behave differently. This is where the rubber meets the road.

ALEX: You've said this to me before about behaviors, but I'm tempted to just let things play out for a while. Don't you agree with me that today felt like a real step forward? Like a watershed—maybe now that the leadership team "gets it," we'll see some big changes around here.

KATZ: If you stopped now, you'd make a classic mistake. But don't feel bad—it's exactly the same error most leaders in your shoes make: declaring victory too soon. It's not enough to get leaders to develop insight about the culture. Of course it's great that the people in the room today—Ross, Travis, Florence, Avery, all the rest—have a deeper insight about what motivates people at Intrepid. But now you need to connect this understanding to new ways of acting, both for them and for other people. You need to get down to the level of behaviors so you can build more emotional energy and commitment around those behaviors.

ALEX: Give me an example. I'm a tactical guy. Tell me what that would look like.

KATZ: Well, the topic of the former green initiative came up a couple of times. Avery brought it up after the discussion about Calvin's departure as another example of something that he believes is "broken" here at Intrepid. Did you catch that?

ALEX: Yes, that was interesting. I didn't know that he and his marketing team had put so much work into Toby's green campaign. He was clearly very disappointed that it hadn't gone anywhere.

KATZ: Imagine if that initiative, instead of being a top-down one based on posters on the wall, had evolved from the trenches, from the real ways that people worked. Then you might have seen real commitment: emotional alignment, not just rational compliance.

ALEX: [*Looking skeptical*] Are you saying the green initiative could have transformed our culture? That sounds too easy—like we're leaving aside the question we started with: how do we get the whole organization to be nimble, to move into the twenty-first century?

KATZ: That is not what I'm saying. Culture is a much broader issue than companies just doing good. If Intrepid's culture were better aligned with its strategic and operational priorities, it would be easier for a leader to design something like a green initiative to be practical, "sticky," and self-sustaining. And it would also be easier for leaders to design other initiatives, like a cybersecurity one, that had more than a snowflake's chance in heck of making it off the ground—because they could ask, "How do we do this in a way that goes with the grain of how our people behave and what they feel good about doing, rather than working against it?"

ALEX: I see. That sounds like a great idea, but how does something like that happen? What's the path?

KATZ: The path forward is not unlike the work you've been doing since we began a few months ago. Again, I'm asking you to look within your organization, to find what's best and strongest and what generates positive emotional responses from your people. You ask people at all levels across the organization about how they do their work every day. You find behaviors that are already being performed today that represent the best of Intrepid. You ferret out the feelings that are generated by these behaviors. Then you have the discipline to select and connect the "critical few" behaviors with those feelings that will provide balanced motivation over time.

ALEX: Okay. You go wide, and then you go deep. And you keep these conversations moving toward an end goal. That is beginning to make sense to me, but it also sounds like a ton of work! How do I do all this and keep running the company as well? [*He glances at his phone, as if the sheer weight of all the unanswered emails from the day is pulling his eyes toward the table.*]

KATZ: I actually think it would be worthwhile to hand over key elements of this undertaking to a few of your leadership team members—the critical few who already seem to be on board—and to let them run with it. Florence and Travis feel obvious; Avery might be an unconventional choice, but sometimes a cynic can be useful. It's worth talking to him one-on-one. But you don't want this to be just a leadership effort. You want to engage people further down and make them part of the movement. You can also use this as a way of enabling collaboration among leaders who seldom have a chance to work together in their formal roles.

[*Katz slows down as he finishes, noticing that he's lost Alex's attention to his phone. Alex looks up, apologetic, and holds up a finger as if to speak. Just at that moment there's a knock on the conference room door, and Florence comes in, clearly excited.*]

FLORENCE: I have some fantastic news—guess who just called and asked if he could have his job back? Calvin! The e-commerce company wasn't a fit. He'd like to be back at Intrepid, if we'll have him.

ALEX: I just saw that email and was about to tell Katz. If you'll both excuse me, I'm going to step out and give him a call. [*He leaves the room.*]

KATZ: That's amazing! I look forward to meeting him; Alex has said great things. You look concerned, though.

FLORENCE: I've hired a replacement for him—she started last month and is really digging in. I don't know that I have room for him in my budget. [*Alex reenters. He clearly seems keyed up and a little distracted, but he enters smoothly back into the conversation.*]

KATZ: I have an unconventional suggestion, and I think Alex will be on board. [*He looks at Alex, and they smile and nod at each other.*] Bring Calvin on in a special projects role, and have him run the cultural alignment efforts for the next few months until you see where his next role will be. He's clearly the kind of guy who speaks truth to power and has the respect of people on the leadership team. Maybe he could spearhead an initiative for evolving the culture.

FLORENCE: [*Looking curious*] So the cultural effort is a thing now? I'd like to be part of it also.

ALEX: I fully support that. Let's figure it out. Florence, let's set up some time tomorrow. We have real work to do. Katz, I'm not sure we're done with you yet—please don't go too far.

KATZ: I've got plans to see my granddaughter's dance performance this weekend, but I've decided to stick around the rest of the week—I hear that lamb chops are the special at Casimir's this evening, and I'd love to keep chatting. Why don't we get together in a few hours?

Change Behavior First

Any leader who, like Alex, is struggling to understand how to harness emotional energy to drive priorities faces a basic challenge: How do you go from diagnosing to *directing*? Once you develop a clear, outside-in, nuanced perspective on the tendencies and inclinations within your organization today, how do you encourage that culture to evolve in a new direction? What are the ways to get more people to participate in the human interactions that will drive business results? How do you go from just talking about how things *should* happen to actually getting people in key places to take actions that yield better results?

We believe that there are specific ways to intervene in corporate cultures—to take tangible steps that not only accelerate near-term business results but also help support real, lasting culture evolution. It is important to recognize that lasting culture evolution is slow and steady at best. However, it is also important to note that successful, long-term organizational change efforts include simple, clear changes in specific behaviors. And the more these changes become habitual with respect to *keystone habits*, a term coined by writer Charles Duhigg (more on him in a minute), the better. Employees aren't necessarily aware that they're affected by a culture change effort. But they know that they are going to act in some new way at work, that the change is permanent, and that there's a reason for it. A new practice, day by day, can become habitual, rewarding, and socially encouraged instead of labored, sporadic, and discouraging.

Our belief is supported by research in the fields of both management and neuroscience, as well as our own decades of hands-on client work. And it can all be boiled down to one of Katz's most beloved quotes, attributed to Richard Pascale, coauthor of *The Power of Positive Deviance*: "People are much more likely to act their way into a new way of thinking than to think their way into a new way of acting."

This is the key to the kind of behavior change that will enable an organization to evolve to a more coherent, strategy-supporting culture. To illustrate, let's return to the Kate Dugan story from chapter 2. The partner on Kate's project encouraged her to try something new by aligning the action—in this case, facilitating a senior meeting—to a trait she had an emotional connection to, "sleeves rolled up." Why was this effective? He encouraged her to challenge herself by appealing to her natural human desire to feel connected with a larger group. He delineated for her the way that her individual act would align and connect her to an appealing group characteristic. He also drew a connection between that trait, which resonated with her own value set, and a larger strategic objective of the company: impact on clients.

For Kate, this experience was a positive one. How do we know? Years later, she still recounts this story. It was a moment that mattered to her, emotionally as well as rationally, in the course of her career. Kate has become an adept facilitator, and it's a skill in which she takes great pride, in no small part because she once considered it out of her reach. She has repeated and internalized the behavior: it has entered her tool kit, as we say in consulting. It has become, through repetition, ingrained as well as habitual. This is a great example of behavior change and how it operates within the workplace, at the intersection of the individual's personal lived experience and the person's association with, and larger connection to, a greater whole. It also illustrates how change drives and is driven by basic emotions.

The idea that changing behaviors, rather than mind-sets, is the most practical way to intervene in an organization's culture is at the heart of the critical few approach. Charles Duhigg, author of *The Power of Habit: Why We Do What We Do in Life and Business*, writes persuasively about the transformative power of keystone habits. For Duhigg, a keystone habit is "a pattern that has the power to start a chain reaction, changing other habits as it moves through an organization." In other words, if you want to change the way people think, you don't start with or rely primarily on rational argument. You change what they do, even if it doesn't come naturally to them at first. Over time, as the new behavior becomes a pattern, they will likely change how they feel about doing it.

They will see rewards or results of some kind, and those generate positive emotions; those emotions then become associated with the action, encouraging it to be repeated.

In a 2016 piece in the *New York Times*, "How Asking 5 Questions Allowed Me to Eat Dinner with My Kids," Duhigg applies the keystone habits idea. Duhigg's family faced a common problem: their chaotic daily lives made it difficult to sit down to eat together as a family. But instead of throwing up their hands, they approached the aspirational goal of frequent family dinners with the tools of management science. Duhigg applied the classic Toyota Production System technique of the Five Whys—framing the problem and then repeatedly asking "Why?" to uncover root causes. Through this process, the Duhigg family found a root cause of their family disorder: the family was often late getting out the door in the morning because it took so long for the kids to get dressed, triggering a cascade of delays throughout the day. The family developed and agreed on a solution: the children selected and laid out their school clothes the evening before. The net result of this action, the Duhiggs found, was calmer mornings, more productive workdays, and a higher frequency of evening dinners together at home.

Choosing outfits the night before is a perfect example of a keystone behavior, or what psychologists call a "precursor behavior." It is actionable, specific, highly visible, and able to deliver short-term results. It is *viral*—but in this situation, it "infects" and encourages other positive behaviors that collectively helped the Duhiggs accomplish their stated goal. Significantly, it can be tracked and measured. You can imagine a homemade Duhigg family calendar with specific boxes that each child would check each time the clothes were laid out and a star at the end of the week celebrating the number of family dinners they had eaten together. If you can see and celebrate changes, they are far more likely to be repeated. We all, as humans, seek affirmation: we can take advantage of this human trait to encourage behaviors that we want to see repeated.

IMPACT OF CHANGING BEHAVIORS: EXAMPLES FROM OUR WORK

Clearly, an individual, or even a group, can use a behaviors-focused approach to make some desired change, but is it really possible to apply this principle across complex, global organizations? We believe that it is and that the discipline, persistence, and patience that Katz recommends to the fictional Alex is the key to expanding these types of incidents and stories into real, lasting, scalable change. And we believe that our work of the last few decades demonstrates this hypothesis.

A few years ago, James led work with a major oil company on a behaviors program designed to shift elements of its global culture to better align with its strategic objectives. One of these objectives involved an organization-wide need to operate at a slimmer margin. As a way of surfacing potential ideas to accomplish cost savings, platform managers were encouraged to conduct weekly meetings focused specifically on cost-saving ideas: this was much like Duhigg's Five Whys exercise with his family but at a much larger scale.

In these conversations, managers pointed out the monumental operational expense of repairing or even replacing equipment that had been mishandled. As it turned out, many of the frontline people who used these machines on a daily basis simply weren't aware of their costs. Up until this point, they had not connected their individual behavior (how they handled equipment) to their organization's larger goal (managing costs for competitive advantage).

Once this connection had been clarified, the people themselves came up with ideas to better economize. At one site, a frontline employee proposed labeling all the machines with price tags. A discernible drop in repair costs was the immediate result. This early, noticeable impact spurred other observations and new behaviors—for example, one employee then pointed out that the general practice of running cooling fans at all times was superfluous when the temperatures dropped. Thus began a new practice of turning off fans when they weren't necessary, leading to further cost savings. And these ideas then jumped from location to location. Idea by idea, more cost-conscious ways of behaving came into being, spreading organically across the organization. These habit patterns were recognized, acknowledged, and rewarded—and this positive bias led to their repetition. The behaviors moved from one-time acts to ingrained ways of getting things done. Thus, a new way of behaving became more prominent in the overall culture. What previously had been neglected became both a source of pride and the kernel of an idea that spread through peer networks.

In another client example from Katz's work, a telecommunications company was seeking to improve customer service. Prior to our conversations with company leaders, this company had launched countless other efforts to achieve this goal and had seen little impact. Many organizations, we find, begin with the hope that a communications campaign can fit the bill, and this company was no different. But posters on the walls of the call centers urging employees to be polite to disgruntled customers had had little effect. A more intensive effort was made to ferret out the "root cause" by rolling out empathy training for all call center staff, but again, the program did not lead to any discernible difference.

Our work with this company began with intensive conversations with the call center employees themselves—about these failed efforts, yes, but more broadly about the potential value in their daily jobs, what motivated them, what frustrated them, and what helped them get through their most difficult days. It became clear to us that previous efforts had approached the problem as one of *mind-set*—leaders had made the assumption that employees could be mandated or trained to think differently about their customers, to approach interactions with more empathy, and that this empathy would lead to a rise in customer service quality. Leaders were not wrong in believing in the connection between empathy and customer service—indeed, our Katzenbach Center research has demonstrated that customer service companies that embrace an institution-wide ethos of empathy realize a sustainable competitive advantage—but their error was in believing that such a change in perspective could be mandated and controlled, rather than cultivated and encouraged.

We took a different tack. Through our observations of call centers and analysis of their data, we noted that the centers in which customer service scores were high had something notable in common: a markedly positive emotional connection among people on teams. To be more specific, teams that worked well together and enjoyed one another's company also treated customers with more dignity and respect. Changed behavior, habitually sustained, equals changed

mind-set—simple, compelling, and permanent. This observation helped us work with leaders to develop a new approach
to supporting call centers in their customer service empathy:
a training program based on teaming behaviors, which leaders had come to believe were the "root," "keystone," "precursor" behaviors to better customer outcomes.

FROM KEYSTONE TO ORGANIZATION-WIDE BEHAVIORS

What is required to apply this simple concept of keystone behaviors to the transformation of a complex global organization? Time, patience, and the willingness to be selective. To
explain, let's compare the Duhiggs' dinner experiment with
our oil company and telecommunications examples. Imagine
the duration of the Duhigg family experiment: likely, it
played out over a few weeks. To succeed, it required the collective commitment of four people—from the sounds of it,
four busy people, but nevertheless just four. By the end of
a few weeks, they were able to see and understand certain
patterns and therefore could better determine (a) what was
working and (b) how potentially significant this was to the
larger effort to achieve their stated goal of more frequent
family dinners. By contrast, the oil and telecommunications examples, although they follow the same simple logic
and illustrate the same core principles, unfolded over many
months against a backdrop of constant hypothesizing, idea
collecting (and discarding), experimentation, and leadership
alignment. Other ideas bubbled up and proved less effective
(persuasive, actionable, repeatable, realistic) than the clever
price tag and teamwork ideas that ended up in these stories.
Discipline, selectivity, process, and collective commitment

across large groups of leaders at all levels were required to get from a portfolio of new ideas to a few clever ones with the potential for real organization-wide impact, a trial-and-error tolerance to sift through and shake out the critical few. Exhibit 3.1 shows a framework that has been helpful in these types of conversations, making clear what is meant by *behaviors*.

Exhibit 3.1 Explaining behaviors

Many leaders find it hard to pick just a few behaviors to focus on. So they pile one directive on top of another. They overinvest in the pursuit of comprehensive frameworks. They then assume, "With all this effort, all these mandates, surely I'm going to see change now." Their efforts to improve performance remain ill-focused and diffuse; even when efforts are aligned to the same ultimate goal, they can clash with or even undermine one another. In short, most efforts to address and change culture are too comprehensive, programmatic, esoteric, and urgent.

That's why narrowing to a critical few behaviors is essential. Once the behaviors are identified, clarified, and supported, they can strengthen the existing culture. The powerful difference between an alignment approach that focuses on a critical few and an approach that attempts to change a whole culture to align with an external framework lies in the simple act of being selective, the pure, true heart of pragmatism.

So selection is key. But before you can become selective, let's be clear on what we mean when we say "organization-wide keystone behaviors."

DEFINING ORGANIZATION-WIDE BEHAVIORS

Exhibit 3.2 is a brief excerpt from a list of effective organization-wide behaviors we've developed through re-peating the process we've described with clients around the world. Note the primary characteristics they have in common: To begin, they are concise and coherent. They are also directive. Each begins with a verb, and this is deliberate. This syntax choice reflects the ultimate goal for any critical be-havior: it can be acted on. It isn't an emotion, an attitude, or a perception. Although those things are important, they can-not be seen, publicly addressed, or measured; therefore, we don't allow them in this list. The behaviors are also simple. Although they reflect intimate conversations about each cli-ent and how employees work together, they can also be un-derstood by the newest employee.

Have we compiled a comprehensive list of *all* the best behaviors? Have we ranked them to see which are most ef-fective—which will give you the "performance culture," the "aligned culture," or the "innovation culture" you seek? If only we had a dollar for every time we heard those questions! We have disappointing news to share: There are no perfect

Organization-wide behaviors

- Use business goals and the mission to guide day-to-day project work and decisions
- Enable others to make decisions
- Foster explicit conversations about trade-offs between quality, speed, and budget
- Recognize each other for achievements, and back up and support each other
- Give your expert input freely and willingly, but if someone decides to go another way, support him or her
- Create a need for certainty, and do not allow decisions to be reopened
- Get to know others in social settings
- Use a data-driven approach to evaluate risks and be accountable for your recommended solutions
- Name decisions and the facts behind decisions clearly
- Spend more time outside the walls of the office getting to know customers
- Use rigorous internal networking to build cross-organization relationships and pursue mutually beneficial goals
- Look proactively for upstream and downstream implications before making system changes
- Align resources explicitly to prioritized opportunities to maximize impact

Exhibit 3.2 Examples of organization-wide behavior

behaviors. A behavior that is effective at one company may not be effective at another, and behaviors that are especially helpful in one industry may be irrelevant in another.

The good news, however, is that certain behaviors are right for *your* company, *right now*, and if you understand your culture traits, you are likely to uncover them. Traits are neutral; desired behaviors are positive. You will be looking for behaviors that, when encouraged, will move your organization in the direction of your stated aspirations and your strategic intent, all while aligning to those fundamental traits of who you are as a company. This is, in a nutshell, working with rather than against the grain of your culture.

An effective behavior for your company should

- *Harness existing sources of pride or emotional energy to drive intrinsic motivation toward your aspirations.* Sources of pride differ across companies. For example, employees at a mission-based hospital network may be driven by a commitment to patient care. People working for a large, established company may take special pride in being associated with a premium, globally recognized brand that they can boast about to their neighbors. Individuals working at a startup may relish the challenge of creating new things. In the process of understanding your existing culture traits, you should have already gotten a good idea of these sources of emotional energy.

- *Address barriers that get in the way of realizing your aspirations.* For example, while defining your culture traits, you may have identified that consensus-based decision-making prevents you from moving quickly and being at the forefront of innovation. An effective behavior could thus be individuals taking accountability for decisions rather than seeking consensus.

- *Encourage the replication of actions that enable your goals.* If you made a long list of behaviors that are associated with each trait, you have already listed the ones that are most effective. Choose a few to accentuate and add to your long list.

Although not every behavior will accomplish all three of the goals listed above, each behavior should accomplish at least one.

The best way to identify the behaviors that work for your organization is to do this exercise in parallel with the process of agreeing on your culture traits. You will use many of the same sources of information: interviews and focus groups, existing assessments, existing employee engagement surveys, and your own observations. During your detective work, you can compile a comprehensive list of behaviors that you believe have the potential to help the company achieve its aspirations, and then you can commit, with discipline and rigor, to a critical few.

Let's look at a real example to make this tangible. Exhibit 3.3 is excerpted from an analysis we conducted with a multinational organization that was employing the critical few approach to help accelerate a global transformation. Ultimately, through input from leaders at all levels, this company was able to arrive at traits as well as the critical few behaviors. An additional step in the process was the articulation of "aspirations"—in other words, the traits were "who we are today," the aspirations were "who we want to be," and the behaviors were "what we need to do to get there." This company also found it useful to specify how the behaviors would manifest differently at different levels: senior leaders, middle managers, and the front line.

A. Culture Traits	B. Aspirations	C. Critical Behaviors
Delivery focused	Go the extra mile to deliver	*Front Line*: Collaborate with colleagues and peers to solve customer problems *Middle Managers*: Prioritize process improvements that affect outcome *Senior Leaders*: Share feedback and celebrate examples where people have gone the extra mile
Driving to formalization	Stress teamwork; be more inclusive and less hierarchical	*Front Line*: Offer to assist colleagues to get things done; ask questions to understand each other's ideas; respond to requests for assistance promptly *Middle Managers*: Look for opportunities to help other parts of the business; always respond to requests for help and follow through; develop a sense of shared responsibility and goals across teams *Senior Leaders*: Always respond to requests for help and follow through; visibly support cross-functional projects and prioritize their needs

Exhibit 3.3 From traits to behaviors

A chart like this reveals the kind of clarity that comes from rigorous analysis and tough conversations all across a company. The critical behaviors delineated here are not, at first blush, anything magical. Imagine if you walked into a gathering of the leadership team at a random company and said, "Instead of going through the effort to understand our culture, I'm going to save you some time. Let's all, tomorrow, start behaving this way: 'Share feedback and celebrate examples where people have gone the extra mile.'" At best, the leaders might say, "That sounds like a good idea," try it once or twice, and then keep going about their daily routines. What are the chances that this behavior would lead to any outcomes? By way of contrast, consider how this actual client arrived at this list of the critical few. By the time this chart was created, the leadership team had dedicated hours of robust dialogue to conversations about the culture—what was working, what wasn't working. They had addressed difficult issues that had bubbled up through focus groups and interviews with middle managers and frontline folks. They'd created a long list, and then they had narrowed it down— and significantly, in this narrowing, they'd all agreed (as far as it's possible for leaders with divergent perspectives to agree) to focus on these specific behaviors—out of the full world of possible options. They had brainstormed measurable business outcomes that would result if these behaviors changed and discussed how to embed them in different areas of the business. They had looked one another in the eye and committed to hold one another accountable to upholding these behaviors, which included calling others out for failing to demonstrate them.

The point is, the magic lies not in the *content* of each specific behavior but in the process through which it came into being. The process, not the right and only possible answer, is what generates energy and emotional commitment.

Behavior Development: The Long List

As previously discussed, a long list of behaviors will emerge through the process of understanding your company's culture traits. As you conduct the discussions that will allow you to paint a picture of "the way things get done around here," press for and collect behaviors. Make a note of them, and try to keep them positive; look for those that generate positive emotions and connectivity between people. This doesn't mean, however, that every conversation about culture should be a rosy one in which any complaints or frustrations are immediately brushed under the rug. To get to the critical few behaviors, people will almost always go through a brainstorm step where they list their pain points and get specific about what isn't working. Ask questions about what gets in the way of people's best days of work or what keeps all of you, as a company, from achieving what you aspire to. (Ask, "What keeps us from being more innovative?" "What gets in the way of our processes' working more smoothly?") Move quickly beyond the negative, though. Lingering too long in the "complaining about the culture" stage will simply reinforce behaviors you're trying to change by drawing attention to them and will associate the culture effort you're undertaking with the idea that you can fix what's broken.

Focus next on identifying the positive behaviors that can move your company forward. Look for what is already happening on its own. Remember our example of the telecommunications company—how customer service scores already were high in pockets in the organization? Find and probe these pockets. Consider the entire enterprise carefully. Somewhere in your organization, individuals or teams already manifest the types of behaviors that, if practiced more consistently more of the time, would help your organization accomplish its goals. Managers are empowering employees, encouraging them to see mistakes as learning opportunities. Team leaders are promoting and demonstrating collaboration. Leaders are embracing new ideas or championing forms of integrity—for example, refusing to bend the rules in a certain way or getting rid of outmoded rules and practices. Ask yourself, Why did people in these places behave differently from people elsewhere in the enterprise? Take stock of these positive behaviors and consider which could be harnessed to help others make desired changes.

How can you tell they're the right behaviors? Because they fit closely with the traits that have already been identified. If you look at your long list, you should see how every behavior is relevant to your existing culture, either by strengthening something that is working or addressing something that is not supporting your strategic goals. In addition, these behaviors should make a difference in any significant geography where you operate and in multiple functions and levels.

Behavior Selection: The Critical Few

At this stage in the process, you've developed a long list—presumably, ten to fifteen behaviors that meet the criteria outlined above. Now comes the fun (and the extremely challenging) part: selecting from your long list to attain the critical few. Exhibit 3.4 is a high-level view of how the selection process works; specifics will follow.

We've seen different approaches be effective here. One common way is to plot the behaviors using the axes of effort to implement and impact, as shown in exhibit 3.5.

LONG LIST of Critical Behaviors	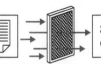	SHORT LIST of Critical Behaviors

Start with the long list of critical behaviors and prioritize them according to a set of criteria

Select three to five critical behaviors for implementation

Potential Prioritization Criteria

Leadership Support
- Will senior leadership adopt and role-model the behavior?

Impact/ Relevance
- Will the behavior impact the most critical areas/business objectives?

Impact on Motivation
- Does the behavior change create motivation and momentum for follow-up efforts?

Duration to Impact
- Will the targeted behavior change lead to visible impact quickly?

Ease of Implementation
- Can the targeted behavior change be implemented without other major changes (e.g., changes to performance management system)?

Measurability
- Can the targeted behavior change be measured/tracked?

Visibility
- Does the behavior display a high degree of symbolism that can quickly be recognized?

Spread
- Is the behavior change likely to go viral (e.g., because it makes people's jobs easier)?

Exhibit 3.4 Prioritization of critical behaviors

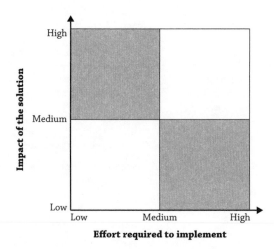

High

Medium

Impact of the solution

Low

Low Medium High

Effort required to implement

Exhibit 3.5 Effort to implementation versus impact

This is a simple two by two framework that encourages a conversation about trade-offs and requires realism about what can be accomplished. Other organizations use a voting process, which can vary from the public and very low tech, like a simple show of hands, to the private and electronic, like a voting tool.

Working with clients around the globe, we've observed that there is no perfect way to get from the many to the few. Indeed, the process that clients choose usually reflects (and teaches us about) how information is processed and decisions are made within that particular culture. For example, in our work with a financial services firm in Asia, we quickly realized that the leaders had a strong preference for visual representations of the behaviors that emphasized how much data and analysis had gone into their development. This made the decision feel less impulsive to them, more data driven and precise. Therefore, for the leadership meeting where the critical few behaviors were selected, we papered the walls with large posters similar to what you see in exhibit 3.6.

The posters contained highlights of what we'd heard in interviews and focus groups, which clarified why each behavior would benefit the organization as a whole. They also suggested more specific behaviors that could apply at every level. Leaders spent their time together walking around the room, considering and discussing each behavior. This helped them feel, when they made the ultimate choice of just three behaviors, that they'd made a decision fully supported by data. By contrast, an entertainment company in a turnaround situation dedicated a few hours of its leadership team meeting to vociferous open debate and then quickly came to a consensus with a show of hands—consistent with the "get it done right away" trait that we'd noticed in the company's culture.

Why the emphasis on just "a few"? And how will you know that you've chosen the right behaviors? The first question is easy to answer: because you need somewhere to begin. Changing everything at once is impossible. Focusing on just a few behaviors allows for consistency and coherence. You are, in essence, about to undertake a science experiment with your company, and just as with a science experiment, you need to establish a framework that will allow you to see and document results.

The second question is also easy to answer, but you might not want to share this information with the full leadership team before you try getting them to have a real discussion about choices: there are no perfect few behaviors. Likely, if you have been thorough and thoughtful in developing the long list, any of the behaviors would be useful and effective in moving your culture forward. The process deciding which

What we heard

Insights from interviews with senior executives,
middle managers, and frontline staff

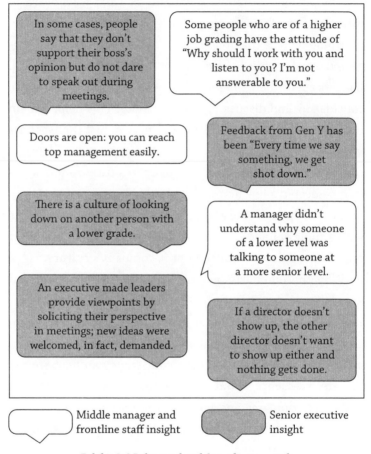

Exhibit 3.6 Behavior detail from client example

ones to prioritize is, in and of itself, a form of intervention. By deciding on and committing to these behaviors together, you and your colleagues are taking a big step toward making your culture stronger and more coherent.

Behavior: "Value performance over seniority"; be more inclusive and less hierarchical

Senior Leaders. . .

- ask colleagues who are less senior in grade for their opinions in meetings and acknowledge their contribution
- openly thank junior staff for results achieved
- have an "open door" and regularly leave their office to talk to middle and frontline staff
- directly seek feedback and input from frontline staff

Middle Managers. . .

- encourage junior colleagues to voice their opinions in meetings and acknowledge their contribution
- contribute their ideas in senior forums and create opportunities where junior staff members can contribute their ideas
- relay achievement of a junior staff member to senior leaders and tell the junior staff member this occurred

Team Members. . .

- volunteer to work and liaise with people of all grade levels
- speak up to offer opinions when senior colleagues are present
- encourage and support their colleagues to contribute ideas in senior forums

Exhibit 3.6 (continued)

WALKING THE TALK: SYMBOLIC ACTS

In conversations with leadership teams about behaviors, one of the most powerful moments usually occurs when one leader turns to another and says, "What will you do differently, starting today?" The best leaders demonstrate the selected behaviors every day and at every opportunity. When the company leadership steps up and walks the talk, people take notice and then take action. All of an organization's members should be expected to embed behaviors into their daily work, but those seen as leaders have both an opportunity and an imperative to do so in a way that catches people's attention and sends a strong message that things are changing around the workplace.

A symbolic act is a deliberate, purposeful action taken by the leadership that sends a strong archetypal message. Symbolic acts can be undertaken by an individual leader or by a leadership team as a collective. What's important is that they are explicitly designed and executed in a way that sends a message coherent with the overall culture evolution. For example, a collective symbolic act at a global airline client was the leadership decision to break the tradition of holding all leadership team meetings at the headquarters in Australia and to instead rotate the location every quarter across each of the continents the airline served. Significantly, this was not done quietly behind the scenes. This change in practice was announced by the CEO to the full organization, with an explicit connection made between this choice and the new behavior: "incorporate a global perspective in all major decisions." At each quarterly meeting, local representatives were invited to attend and to provide a local perspective. It was a simple act with far-reaching implications.

In another example from our client work, the CEO of an investing firm made a bold and uncomfortable decision: he shared the full results of his 360-degree feedback with the rest of his team, warts and all. This was a way of demonstrating, visibly, that the goals the team had discussed of transparency and emotional commitment could be accomplished only when each person decided to take a step beyond his or her comfort zone. Other members of the leadership team emulated his action, sharing their own feedback. This is an example of an act going viral—with, again, very long-term implications for shifting the culture of this firm toward more trust and collaboration.

Another firm's CEO chose to interpret one of his organization's critical behaviors, "respect each other," by drawing up a list of behaviors that he promised to practice with regularity: avoid personal remarks, never interrupt, and pay close attention to what everyone said. He also, in a move that reflected the same purposeful humility as the investing firm CEO's gesture of sharing his 360-degree feedback, asked a few informal leaders on his team to call his attention privately to any of his notable hits and misses. This move likely caused him some discomfort, especially at first, but it had a powerful effect on his organization's culture.

One of Katz's all-time favorite examples of a symbolic act comes from the military. Alfred M. Gray is a United States Marine Corps general who served as an important leader throughout the turbulent, post-Vietnam 1970s and served as twenty-ninth commandant from 1987 to 1991. Gray is known for effecting a transformation sometimes called "the second enlightenment of the Marine Corps"; changes that are attributed to Gray include the emphasis on Marine Corps service as a leadership development opportunity and the establishment of a Marine Corps University. Formal photographs of Gray feature him in battle fatigues, not a dress uniform. Those outside the military might not understand how bold a message this sent: it emphasized the core ethics that Gray sought to build in the corps, including mutual respect and what he called the "warrior spirit." And this was not simply a formal posture for photographs. Gray wore these fatigues at all times and entered mess halls without any insignia to eat the same meals as his Marine Corps privates.

In one CEO's early days at the helm of a prominent technology company, the chief was lauded in the press for tearing down the fence around executive parking and taking an annual salary of $1. These were symbolic acts, to be sure—notable, as with Gray, for demonstrating humility. In our days working with the company under this CEO's leadership, we also heard of a notable symbolic act that was powerful in how it demonstrated not just the chief's own humility but the desire to redirect others toward new, more effective ways of behaving. Whether walking the halls meeting employees or hunkered down with the leadership team, the CEO regularly posed a question: "What are your competitors doing?" This would send employees scrambling to look outside the company's walls and better understand the market—a behavior that the chief executive wisely understood as key to making a behemoth organization more nimble and outward facing. Core to this symbolic act was its element of repetition; because the CEO did it not once but repeatedly over time, a shift in behaviors was encouraged. Undoubtedly, people who had this experience told others about it and caused those others to work to understand competitors as well. Who, after all, would want to run into the CEO and not have a good answer to that one pointed question?

As different as these examples are, they all had a notable impact on the people in the organizations in which the leaders served—they catalyzed and deepened emotional commitment to both the organization overall and to the leader as an individual. This kind of emotional commitment, over time, helps each person take similar chances, to act and behave in new ways that might feel unnatural at first but ultimately become rewarding and self-reinforcing. When people can feel an emotional as well as rational alignment between their company's identity and purpose and their own individual behaviors, they feel connected; when that sense of connection is attached to the organization's ability to reach its goals, the organization has a culture that is working for and supporting its purpose.

4. A Few Authentic Informal Leaders

SCENE: *Mid-May, the evening of the same day as the leadership meeting. Back at Casimir's.*

ALEX: I'm glad you didn't leave town right away and were willing to meet up again. And I also appreciate that you don't mind coming back to the same restaurant.

KATZ: I'm a creature of habit, particularly when it comes to good food. And I'm happy to be helpful—it feels like you're on the brink of doing something really important for Intrepid, and that's always worth my time. But tell me what got you so riled up at the end of our meeting today—I think that something bigger than Calvin's return is on your mind.

ALEX: I won't beat around the bush, Katz. One of our board members, Sebastian, had sent me an email that said we had to discuss something urgent. I spoke to him right before dinner. You know how we've been struggling to develop an e-commerce strategy? The board seems to think that acquiring a small local startup in this space could be the answer, and they have suggested that I meet with their founder and start to think it through.

KATZ: [*Raises his eyebrows*] That *is* news. How do you feel about it?

ALEX: I have mixed feelings, of course. I'm already struggling to make all the different parts of the current company work together and be in sync; the idea of bringing
in some new entity seems like it might be the thing that
tips us over into total chaos. I'm also proud that the
board thinks that we're up to this and supports the idea
of real investment.

[*Alex looks far away, as if trying to see into the future;
then, with visible effort, he focuses again on the topic at
hand.*]

What would a prospect like this do to our conversation about culture, though? Should we hit the pause but-
ton until I figure this one out? Does it make sense to try
to understand Intrepid today if Intrepid might change so
dramatically in the future?

KATZ: Let's not jump so far ahead yet—let's keep to where
we are today.

ALEX: Because the deal might fall through anyway?

KATZ: That, of course, but not just that. Let's say that you
knew with certainty today that you'd be integrating with
another company. Do you know why most mergers fail?

ALEX: Culture issues, I imagine.

KATZ: Yes, that's right—clashes in working styles, disparate
ways of behaving, different sources of emotional energy.
Integrations are always grounded in rational reasons,
and then the irrational, emotional side of an organization refuses to fall in line. A new org chart makes perfect
sense on paper but asks people to work in ways that they
aren't accustomed to, that go against the grain of what
they liked about their previous job. It's very common.
Whether or not you should acquire this startup isn't just

a question of whether it aligns with Intrepid's strategy or whether you can afford it—it's also a question of how well the cultures will mesh.

ALEX: That makes sense to me—but how am I going to figure that out?

KATZ: You just stay the course of what you're doing.

ALEX: But now I have this much more urgent deadline. How can I accelerate my understanding of Intrepid's culture?

KATZ: Let's back up a little bit. I want to remind you of something we discussed the last time we were here, over lunch in January. Remember that you told me you were spending more time walking around all the offices and the distribution centers, just having casual conversations. Are you still making time to do that?

ALEX: [*Looking pleased*] Absolutely. Why do you ask?

KATZ: I was thinking about that guy you mentioned who came up and told you that no one says thank you.

ALEX: Michael, yes; he's a real character. I've made a point of circling back and talking to him a couple more times since then.

KATZ: What have you learned?

ALEX: Michael is in the real estate management group, and he's a bit of an odd fellow. His role involves negotiating terms of leases and land purchases. Considering how slow our growth has been in the last few years, he hasn't been involved in anything that has caught the attention of senior leadership, but he seems to be a genius in terms of how things get done. People turn to him from other departments, even outside real estate. I ran into this new buyer the other day and was asking her how her first few months have been. She told me a story about how she was looking for an expert on forecasting to help her plan for Black Friday, and of course it was Michael who had made the introduction.

KATZ: Is he a name everyone knows at the leadership team level, like Calvin?

ALEX: Absolutely not. I imagine only one or two of the top team would know who he is. Maybe Ross would because he's been here forever and ever. [*Looks thoughtful*] That's probably also true about a lot of the people I've been having lengthy conversations with—they aren't the names we all know. But they are definitely the people who go the extra mile, every day, to get things done.

KATZ: Who else do you put in this category? Anyone else in real estate?

ALEX: No, they're all over the map. We have some in marketing, under Avery, who are doing outstanding work with our online presence. There's an e-commerce guy called Varun who's been making a case that we shouldn't have separate design departments for online and stores. He took it upon himself to set up an informal working group between his team and the store designers. It's exactly the kind of thing that I wish more people would do.

There are also store managers who talk to me, and it's usually the stores with good sales. But not always. There was one store manager, Theo, who everyone said I had to meet. His numbers were pretty poor, but when I talked to him about his territory, I realized that, given the circumstances, he was actually pulling off phenomenal sales—a local employer had just closed its doors, and the whole area was struggling.

KATZ: We have a name for this kind of individual: an authentic informal leader, or AIL. They're the people who are already, in their daily lives and jobs, demonstrating just the kind of behaviors that you want to encourage and promote. And their influence on the feelings and behaviors of those around them is not just a function of their formal role. In addition, many of them are also excellent at sensing and articulating the mood and opinions and emotions of others, so we refer to them as "emotional sensors" as well.

ALEX: Calvin must be an authentic informal leader, right? That's why the whole leadership team is thrilled he's returning.

KATZ: He might be. But to be able to tell, you'd need to validate your impression with the frank opinion of peers and people who work under him. Many leaders presume that their favorites, the so-called high potentials, are the highest-influence people all across the organization. That isn't always the case. Some high performers are also highly influential with people at all levels—but others are more focused on promotion than they are on understanding what motivates their peers. Most leaders don't think to engage AILs who are off the radar of senior management. And they are shortsighted not to do so.

ALEX: I like this AIL idea very much. And I might even be starting to think like you, Katz. So let me tell you what I think you're going to say next.

KATZ: [*Laughing*] I can't wait.

ALEX: These AILs should be my "change champions," right? If we do acquire this startup, I should get them on board

and get them to use their influence to help bring the organization on board, right?

KATZ: Not quite. I actually want you to engage this population much sooner—in fact, I want you to start right
away. Before you ask these AILs to do anything for you,
I want you to listen to them because they understand
how things really work at Intrepid. And the good news
is, if you are rigorous about finding those with unique
emotional capabilities, you can make an excellent start
with no more than a double handful. As the momentum
builds, the AIL groups will flourish and multiply. They
constitute an invaluable "secret weapon" in every successful cultural realignment effort. Remember how I
pressed you to move from behaviors to traits? The AILs
will help you do that. If you choose the right authentic
informal leaders and investigate what it is that makes
them special, you will likely see that they exhibit the behaviors that, if more people did more of them every day,
would be key to helping Intrepid accomplish its goals.

ALEX: Like Varun, the e-commerce guy who set up the working group with the design team.

KATZ: Exactly. Then, as you develop this behaviors list, you
continue to refine it with these AILs, just like you did
with focus groups when you defined Intrepid's traits. But
this time, you can set up an ongoing two-way dialogue
instead of a one-off opportunity to be heard. Monitor the
discussion topics, and follow through on action items—
really let these people know that their input matters.

ALEX: And doing this would be useful, you think—regard-
less of whether or not we decide to go through with the
acquisition?

KATZ: Absolutely. If you *are* going to join forces with another company, you will want to go into that new relationship with a very clear understanding of what it is that makes Intrepid special, what motivates people, and what gets in their way. Imagine yourself in this same restaurant with that other CEO—envision how powerful it would be to be able to say clearly to that other leader, "This is how our culture works, and here's how we can tap what's best in it to take full opportunity of this integration."

ALEX: And should the integration not take place after all?

KATZ: Then you're right back at the same questions that we ended our meeting with today—what are the core traits of Intrepid's culture, and what do we want people to do more of and less of to accomplish our strategic and operating goals? What are the critical few behaviors—and what will it look like, here at Intrepid, if more people exhibit more of these behaviors more of the time?

ALEX: And how will we know if this is working? How would we measure it when these critical behaviors take hold?

KATZ: I absolutely promise you, if you engage the right authentic informal leaders and you connect those behaviors and emotions that help tie human motivation to rational elements of business performance, the way to measure it will be totally clear—you are going to measure what matters to employees as well as customers and shareholders.

ALEX: I'm persuaded—and committed to moving forward. And I think that hostess is now exhibiting the behavior of "eyeing us and wondering when we're finally going to order." Are you ready?

KATZ: Well, one of my personal critical few behaviors is that I always order lamb chops if they're on the menu! Let's eat.

THE POWER OF AUTHENTIC INFORMAL LEADERS

In Katz's decades of work in this field, one of his formative client experiences was his opportunity to advise General Motors as it climbed out of severe financial distress following its declaration of Chapter 11 in June 2009. For CEO Fritz Henderson, harnessing emotional energy to drive GM's change priorities was not an option—it was an imperative. Katz's recollection of early conversations with Henderson are vivid. "Everyone is telling us to change our culture," Henderson lamented. "And people are going to expect to see it happen right away. In fact, they want it to have happened yesterday. Here's the trouble: I know that simply isn't possible. A culture takes shape over decades. This is true anywhere; it is especially true at GM. Our culture is global, complex. It is a challenge just to understand it, let alone to replace it or guide it toward change."

Henderson; GM's head of leadership and culture, Chris Oster; and Katz all agreed on a core premise: General Motors' leaders must work "with and within," rather than against, the strong prevailing culture. The leadership team decided to identify and execute on four top behavior change priorities: speed of execution, sensible risk, clear accountability, and customer service.

To address the speed of execution, Henderson slashed layers of bureaucracy and dismantled multiple product and strategy boards. In their place, he established a single eight-person executive committee that reported to him directly, twice a week. He also established a senior culture council. This council included manufacturing executive Mary Barra, who later became the head of HR and then, eventually, CEO— the first woman to hold that role in US automotive history. One of the culture council's tasks was to find out more about how and where these four priorities were already prevalent across the organization. In other words, just as described in the chapters on traits and behaviors, Henderson took a pragmatic approach. He did not try to change the complex GM cultural situation in its entirety toward some ideal defined by an external framework. Instead, he directed his attention to finding answers within the organization.

Henderson believed that steering GM through turbulent waters required a deep, intuitive understanding of culture. His culture council formed a strategy council of very well-respected informal leaders from the front line and middle management to serve as a sounding board and voice of the people: "Fritz's 50." Members of this group were not the high potentials on a clear path to senior leadership; rather, they were solid citizens, many of long tenure, most at the front line or lower middle management. To find them, the council consulted traditional sources such as HR records and annual reviews. They also sought stories and anecdotes and relied on their own experience and intuition. They cross-checked their list against the opinions of others who had worked directly with the candidates. When the list was narrowed to the initial fifty, the culture council felt confident that they had found a group who represented, and could articulate, the way that people across General Motors were thinking and feeling.

Throughout GM's storied turnaround, Fritz's 50 played a crucial role. They expanded to include other configurations.

These groups gave the CEO and other senior leaders a ground-level, authentic view of the day-to-day challenges that stood in the way of achieving their cultural and behavioral priorities. They were also able to translate the leaders' core messages about GM's need to transform into plain language and emotionally appealing stories that were crystal clear to their peers. This helped generate the kind of emotional support that Henderson and subsequent senior leaders across GM needed to be successful.

At the time of this writing, General Motors is considered one of the great turnaround stories of the last few decades. Sales in 2016 broke records, and the company is currently known for dramatically improved product quality and customer service. While multiple factors were involved in this transformation, Henderson's commitment to focusing on culture as an accelerant to accomplishing goals played an important role. He made a bold choice to activate and empower a group of frontline folks to help make it happen.

Mary Barra, GM's current CEO, has made a commitment to GM's culture a platform of her leadership. In an interview featured at *Fortune*'s 2013 Most Powerful Women Summit, Barra discussed the radical effect that the focus on targeted cultural change following the bankruptcy had on GM's ways of doing business, by reducing policies and slashing bureaucracy. She also made it clear that she believes employee engagement is the key to making sure that GM's recovery continues: "If we win the hearts and minds of employees," she said, "we're going to have better business success."

Every organization has individuals within it whose social capital and emotional intuition set them apart from their peers. Furthermore, these special individuals can play a powerful role in driving positive change. When organizations are undergoing major challenges, such as strategic or operational transformation, engaging authentic informal leaders can help the greater organization accomplish what would otherwise be considered impossible. This is one of this book's most profound and simple truths and a through-line that connects most of Jon Katzenbach's work and writings, from the early 2000s until today.

In the previous chapters, we have referenced these authentic informal leaders several times—they are the kinds of trusted individuals whose opinions and advice should guide you at every stage of your cultural journey. In this chapter, we turn our full focus on AILs: how to recognize them, how to mobilize them, and what impact they can and will have on your effort to transform your organization's culture. Katz loves to describe AILs as akin to special forces in the military, such as the Green Berets and Navy SEALs. Like these elite military units, AILs are subsets of an organization whose relatively small numbers belie their position of influence, thanks not to their formal leadership role but to their total dedication to that organization's mission and purpose. They reflect something strong about the overall traits of the larger whole and are capable of extraordinary acts that could not be managed through the formal organization. And significantly, their special accomplishments open windows that allow the rest of us to see the light, to reconsider what we believe to be possible.

What might AILs look like in *your* organization? How can you find them, and what might you do with them to help you engage your overall culture evolution goals?

Defining an Authentic Informal Leader

Let's start with what they are not: authentic informal leaders are not on your executive team or in any other highly placed position on your organization chart. Formal leaders play a role in any effort to evolve a culture, but their influence and position mean that they are already empowered to do so. By convening AILs, you are seeking to add a new dimension of insight to formal lines of authority, rather than recreate them. Therefore, you want to engage those for whom cultural legitimacy, emotional intuition, and relationship capital are far stronger than they are for others in similar positions.

AILs also aren't your high potentials, the superstar performers who are next in line for formal leadership roles. Most of them do not harbor those aspirations; their basic motivations go well beyond money and position. This is precisely the reason they can add a dimension of influence that complements formal programmatic efforts. In a 2016 *strategy+business* blog post, "How to Find and Engage Authentic Informal Leaders," Reid Carpenter describes how AILs are often especially strong in areas that traditional performance criteria overlook, such as *emotional intelligence* (more on this term later in the chapter). For example, an AIL might prioritize building relationship networks over self-promotion.

An AIL also plays a broader role than the change agents or ambassadors whom organizations enlist to help distribute the cascaded communications messages in conventional change programs. This is not to diminish the role that these conventional ambassadors play in a change effort—much praise is due to those individuals who receive the binder, learn the key points, and get the message out. But a conventional ambassador role presumes that the communication flow is mostly one way; ambassadors are executing on the messages that are issued from on high. An engaged group of AILs is a lot more—how shall we say it?—mouthy. They aren't just there to channel a message—they are there to translate it if they believe in it and also to call foul if they do not and push the leadership to try harder! We believe, based on our work and our research, that a gap often exists between how leaders view their own culture initiatives and how they are viewed by the rest of the organization. According to our recent global survey, 71 percent of CEOs or board members believe that culture is a high priority for leadership, while only 48 percent of those in nonmanagement roles share this point of view. AILs can help leaders understand (and get to the root cause of) the skepticism that lurks in the lower ranks. Their talent for sensing and responding to what others think and feel means that they will choose a way of communicating key ideas that will strike a chord at all levels of the organization.

Given that, an AIL's role can and should be much more reciprocal than that of a traditional change ambassador. As with Fritz's 50, AILs can be an unfiltered voice, giving valuable perspective on how the messages that senior leaders develop in the top boardrooms will (or won't) resonate for those in middle management and frontline roles. They can articulate what appeals to their coworkers on an emotional level. Ideally, you can work with them to codesign specific sets of practices and experiences that will encourage others to explore how their own collective and individual behaviors play a part in moving the organization closer to its overall goal.

At a mining company James worked with in the Middle East, the selected AILs participated in full-day workshops to brainstorm ideas for how the organization-wide behaviors that had been identified by leaders could be enacted and measured. Some of the ideas they developed led to one of the best examples in our work of how a shift in culture can be perceived and even measured over time. This example will be explored in depth in the next chapter, as it's an excellent illustration of how the evolution of behaviors can be measured.

Another crucial difference between AILs and traditional change ambassadors is that the latter are presumed to be willing advocates for the leadership's stated positions. By contrast, AILs might appear, at first glance, to be skeptics or resisters. This does not necessarily reflect a passive-resistant fear of change (although routinely, it is perceived as such by management). On closer investigation, AILs who raise concerns and objections aren't trying to stand in the way. They are trying to move the organization closer to its potential and to protect and fight for what they understand to be important to people. If you can learn to tell the difference between AILs and malcontents and hear what the former have to say, you will add fuel to your arsenal of ideas and opportunities for how to work with your culture's existing emotional strengths.

A powerful example of a leader who actively engaged the perspective of AILs is Aetna's CEO, Mark Bertolini. Since assuming the CEO role in 2010, Bertolini has navigated the organization through a market of great complexity, including the company's response to the Affordable Care Act and the lead-up to the integration with CVS announced in December

2017. In 2015, in a move that presaged similar moves among other CEOs, Bertolini raised the minimum wage at Aetna for all 5,700 employees to $16 per hour, more than double the federal baseline. This represented an 11 percent pay hike across all 5,700 employees; for some populations, the raise was as high as 33 percent. Simultaneously, Aetna enriched medical benefits for these same workers. Interestingly, in an interview that Katz, Art Kleiner, and Gretchen conducted with Bertolini shortly after this announcement, he credited this decision to the strong (and often critical) voices of front-line employees that he'd solicited across his organization, both through face-to-face conversations and through social media. At the time, Bertolini told us with pride that he was one of the few Fortune 100 CEOs who kept a personal presence on Twitter and said that one of his primary goals as a leader was to have a style that was "approachable, real, and tangible." From his AILs, Bertolini heard a clear message: they were struggling, health care was not affordable to them, and income inequality was a real constraint for them. "After we looked at a number of options to help our lowest-paid employees, I finally said, 'How about we just pay them more?'" he explained.

Certainly, this is an extreme example; not every organization can provide generous raises to all its lowest-paid staff. What's significant is how Bertolini arrived at this formal compensation decision specifically by accessing and listening to voices from across the organization. He was relentless about not just probing the people congratulating and agreeing with him but also seeking out those who dared to speak tough truths. Through his accessible social media presence and his walk-the-halls personal style, he was able to encourage, directly respond to, and give credence to these diversely credible voices. And then, by being articulate in the press about how his own employees' critiques and complaints had spurred him to take this notable, press-worthy decision, he got a surprisingly powerful cultural boost—a burst of positive energy across the organization, a series of integrated moments when employees at all levels felt positive energy connections about their affiliation with the organization. In Bertolini's own telling of the story, it's clear that he was conscious of and cultivated the emotional impact that this announcement would have on his frontline workforce. So initially he broke the news not to shareholders or the press but at a town hall in Jacksonville, Florida, at Aetna's largest call center. "The place exploded," he told us. "I had known that people would be happy, but I wasn't ready for the raw emotion. There were people saying, 'Praise the Lord, my prayers have been answered.'"

This is also a beautiful example of a symbolic act, as we discussed in chapter 3. It was deliberate and purposeful. Everyone in the room who witnessed it came away with a story to tell. And most important, what Bertolini said and how he said it were coherent with the overall message he wanted to convey about the organization's continued commitment to caring for its employees—a force Jon Katzenbach has long watched and written about over the years as the power of "Mother Aetna."

AIL Types

All AILs are able to interpret and harness the emotional tides present in any organization. This idea is premised on Daniel Goleman's concept of EQ, as popularized in his 1995 book, *Emotional Intelligence.* Goleman focuses on high EQ as a leadership trait, arguing that EQ matters twice as much to the success of top leaders as pure intellect or technical expertise. When we describe AILs as "emotional sensors," we are referencing their ability to sense not just the feelings of other specific individuals but the collective feelings of the organization as a whole. This gives AILs the power to anticipate and understand how and why a "rational" leadership decision, like eliminating a flextime arrangement that few employees had taken advantage of, might trigger a negative and unexpected emotional response. (People like to *believe* that their work is flexible, even if they personally find it more effective to work side by side with their colleagues in the office.) AILs have a sense of what emotions will likely be lurking just below the surface, and how and why a leadership decision might stir them up. They can help explain and articulate the elements in an organization that require particular attention.

Some organizations find it useful to categorize specific types of AILs. In our research and experience, we have seen the following:

- *Pride builders.* These are people who can help you design ways to motivate others. They're often frontline leaders or middle managers. Although not often recognized by the formal elements of the organization, these individuals are natural energizers of the system around them. They bring out the best in others. They can make people feel good about the work itself—no matter how boring, grungy, or stressful it may be—by connecting it to something larger than themselves.

- *Exemplars.* Exemplars model effective behaviors. Their actions appeal to others and drive results because these people exhibit behaviors that resonate with the goals of the enterprise. This doesn't necessarily mean following written rules. It means working above and beyond the rules to attain business results. In a hotel or office complex, for example, a front-desk staffer who takes the time to understand incoming customers and identify who in the organization could best answer their questions becomes an example to others—particularly in an organization seeking to promote excellent customer service.

- *Networkers.* These AILs cultivate and nourish informal social connections, enabling important and productive work outside the lines of the formal hierarchy. They are high in what economists and sociologists call "social capital." Networkers, like pride builders, positively influence the overall performance of those around them; also like pride builders, they do not rely on formal position or authority. Networkers know how to accomplish strategically important tasks within the existing culture, even when others find roadblocks. They are often already the hubs of informal networks and therefore stand out easily in well-designed network analysis surveys.

Finding Your AILs

You can find the most effective subpopulations of authentic informal leaders using a variety of methods, ranging from informal conversations to more digitally enabled methods of surfacing patterns of relationships and affiliations such as social network analysis. All these methods have a crucial factor in common: they differ from the formal HR mechanisms used to identify the top candidates for strategic moves or promotions.

In recent years, we have been supporting a complex global banking firm through an ambitious culture evolution. This firm has selected three organization-wide behaviors. The culture team designed a sample ten-question survey. It includes questions about the behaviors themselves ("Do you see these behaviors in action?"), as well as about people who tend to manifest them ("Whom do you know who embodies these behaviors?"). The survey was distributed to more than fifty thousand employees across multiple countries. The how questions will be a pulse survey, repeated over time, which will allow the company to trace how and whether these desired behaviors increase as time goes on. The who questions reveal the AILs, a subgroup of individuals who, through this survey, have been nominated by their peers. Five percent of the population of the bank scored highly on this survey; the culture team validated that list through interviews and comparisons with performance evaluation data. Through this "pressure testing," they gained confidence that the survey had produced an accurate snapshot of the informal leaders across the organization. We then worked directly with these AILs to develop the interventions that will help support and enable the critical behaviors organization-wide.

This bank created a customized survey to unearth the AILs and intends to keep using this survey as a dashboard to track and measure the evolution of the culture. Other organizations have used preexisting data to select AILs. As part of a broad culture transformation effort we engaged in at a technology company, we worked with the vice presidents of HR and global employee engagement to identify and engage a cadre of informal leaders across the full company population. At the time, the employees numbered several hundred thousand, so it was an ambitious goal. The company deployed an annual employee survey called Voice of the Workforce (VoW), which was broader in scope than a traditional engagement survey. Most surveys of this type we've encountered are fully anonymous. This company's VoW was not. But it did not ask respondents to identify themselves; rather, they were asked to identify their direct manager prior to answering any questions about that manager's interactions with them.

By narrowing our focus to just a handful of statements that struck us as behavioral, such as "my manager encourages me to speak openly and honestly even when the news is bad," we were able to produce a list that, we hypothesized, captured the same type of individuals who would have emerged if we'd taken a fully qualitative, interview-based approach. This approach was highly successful; after a first round where we took random samples of the identified individuals and used our customary interviews to test the result, we ended up moving forward with this data-driven approach, allowing the program to scale quickly across continents.

Using tools such as social network analyses or engagement surveys to find your AILs isn't always necessary. (In fact, what we like best about the technology company example is its inherent thrift: the data that the culture team used was already being captured by the organization.) Leaders from the organizations in the examples above found these solutions effective because they wanted to locate and catalyze their networks quickly at a global scale. Depending on size, geographical composition/diffusion of your organization, and countless other factors, you might choose an approach based wholly on thoughtful dialogues with your leadership team, supplemented by targeted interviews.

Exhibit 4.1 lists interview questions that might be useful, based on the qualities you're seeking in your AILs.

Any process or method should help you organize, synthesize, and pressure-test the collective intuition of a range of people from across your organization. This helps you get to an accurate answer, of course. It also helps the process itself send a message that you, like Mark Bertolini in the Aetna example above, are open and willing to listen to a multiplicity of voices and are working hard to get to an answer that's best for your whole company.

Below are some pointers to help you begin.

1. *Use your networks to seek recommendations—and encourage others to do the same.* Start with your direct team. You might hear another leader say, "I've got somebody on my team who seems to demonstrate what we're doing with this critical few." Send emails to colleagues, describing the kind of person you're looking for, and ask for suggestions. Ask your team to do the same. Like Alex, you can also walk the halls and ask people about who energizes them, whom they turn to for information.

2. *Consider your critical few behaviors as a starting point.* In describing the AILs you want to recruit, keep your desired behaviors in mind. You're looking for the informal leaders who "see it" (recognize the value of

AIL Characteristics	Sample Interview Questions
Pride and Purpose. Clarifies exactly what matters and why it matters, again and again	• What makes your team proud to work here? How do you tap into these sources of pride?
Motivation. Builds confidence and spreads positive energy around achieving high performance objectives	• How do you motivate or inspire your team to perform above and beyond expectations? Does that change during difficult periods (e.g., crises)?
Empowerment and Engagement. Shows trust in teammates by delegating expanded responsibility and checks in to course correct, not micromanage	• How do you get to know your team as individuals and not just as colleagues? • How do you empower the team/individuals to take action?
Performance: Accountability and Recognition. Clearly articulates goals and responsibilities and steps in to coach teams who do not meet expectations; celebrates day-to-day successes and personalizes recognition	• How do you make sure everyone knows what's expected of him or her to get the job done? • When your team or an individual is not on pace to hit a goal, how do you approach the situation? • When your team or an individual hits or surpasses a goal, how do you recognize the success or celebrate the win?
Communication. Keeps the team in the loop as new announcements and decisions are made, taking time to explain how they will impact the team's work	• How do you help your team understand new decisions or policies? • What channels, either formal or informal, do you find most effective for ensuring awareness and understanding, and under which circumstances?

Exhibit 4.1 Questions to ask potential AILs

change), "get it" (understand the reasons), "want it" (are committed to change), and, in most cases, already "breathe it." People who have these qualities tend to be recognized by their colleagues as credible, trustworthy, and effective leaders. Then, don't forget about the behaviors when it comes time to announce and recognize the individuals. Reference the behaviors they exemplify, including telling stories about exceptional things they've done and how these acts were manifestations of the behaviors. This is true coherence: when a leader makes use of every step and stage in the culture evolution process to underscore, emphasize, and recognize specific behaviors.

3. *Seek and explore the pockets where expectations are being exceeded.* Remember the telecom example in the previous chapter? The leaders pinpointed call centers with customer service results that exceeded expectations. They then observed those specific centers and came to understand how the keystone behavior of teaming drove high customer satisfaction. Seek your company's pockets of excellence—especially those where success defies logic, like Alex's example of the store that was located in a community that had experienced layoffs but nevertheless managed respectable sales. It's likely that AILs are driving this performance.

4. *Start with "ideal" candidates.* To establish an effective initial group, you must carefully select, develop, and test your informal leaders. Begin with the best of the best. Even if initial efforts turn up only a dozen people who meet the criteria you've defined, that's enough to start. Resist the temptation to rush to a decision here for the sake of expedience. If that first group isn't

carefully composed, the effort will rarely be sustainable over time. The initial group can sharpen your insights about the critical few culture traits to build on
and the critical few behaviors needed to go forward.

5. *Start subtle and then celebrate.* Keep the selection process under the radar, but announce the selection with
appropriate fanfare and acknowledgment. At a recent
client engagement, the selected AILs were all notified
not by an email but through a face-to-face meeting
with their manager. Then, they were invited to a cel-
ebratory breakfast with leaders of both their business
unit and the culture program. These extra efforts on
the part of the culture program leaders ensured that
the AILs understood their selection as a real honor.
And because they were, by definition, highly net-
worked people whom others trusted, their pride at
being acknowledged became a viral force that com-
manded the attention of others. By the "second wave"
of AIL identification, other people were clamoring to
be included.

6. *Encourage viral spread.* After several meetings, the first
group can expand. They should enlist the next informal leaders. At James's mining client in the Middle
East, the first wave of identified AILs all identified
and invited the second wave of participants, which
gave the evolving network a communal feel. The best
informal leaders usually have a strong instinct for rec-
ognizing others who meet similar criteria and can follow their lead.

MOVING AIL NETWORKS TO ACTION

Work with AILs should be ongoing throughout your culture evolution process, taking the form of a series of discussions. You will ask for AILs' feedback on leaders' ideas. You will also ask them how they achieve their goals. Working with the energy of AILs is the best place to dig into cultural obstacles and to determine how you can align strategy, operating model, and culture. AILs are also the very best source of ideas for how to attach the high-minded aspirations of any culture program to real, tangible business results.

The days we convene AILs are always the most satisfying days. These are rollicking, enjoyable sessions. The emotional energy is palpable and contagious. Gathering AILs together amplifies their knowledge and emotional reach—to one another, to senior leaders, and to the wider organization. Participants take renewed energy back to the front line.

These don't sound like conventional change management meetings, do they? The agendas for these sessions tend to be loose; the participants are not expected to walk out of the room and parrot a message from the leaders. Instead, critical issues come to the surface on their own, often with far-reaching consequences. Sincere interest in people's day-to-day work reveals emotionally compelling issues and emotionally charged values, and people tend to find them bracing, thought-provoking, and memorable.

5. Measuring Cultural Action

SCENE: *Mid-October. Alex's office. Calvin, Florence, Elin, and Alex are talking enthusiastically.*

ALEX: Calvin, that's an amazing photo! I can't wait to show it to Katz.

[*Katz knocks and enters.*]

We were just talking about you. Or rather, talking about some of the authentic informal leaders and some of the great things they're up to.

KATZ: I'm sure they are much more interesting than I am! Certainly, they have a lot more wisdom about Intrepid. Tell me what you're all talking about—I can tell I walked in at the good part.

CALVIN: Well, just as you suggested, we found and launched some initial groups of our best authentic informal leaders and started to convene them on a regular basis: first to come up with behaviors and then to identify some areas of the business where these behaviors would make a real difference to results. It was a little counterintuitive at first, but it turned out to be easier than anticipated.

KATZ: Terrific. How have those sessions been?

FLORENCE: They've been "rollicking" discussions, to use one of your favorite words. The more cross-functional the group, the more energetic the discussions and ideas. One of the best sessions so far was with a handful of frontline store employees, some people from marketing, and someone from my supply chain team.

KATZ: Have you taken the behaviors back to the leadership team? And how difficult was it to align them on the critical few?

ALEX: We had a leadership team meeting in early July where we moved from about a dozen behaviors down to three: those are—[*Pulls out a sheet of paper and hands it to Katz*]

KATZ: [*Reading aloud*] "Where processes don't work, focus on fixing them or making them more flexible.

"Respond to what the customers want, based on both quantitative analysis and what we can see and feel.

"Communicate openly; prioritize transparency over a 'need to know' approach."

These are great, really granular and specific. [*Calvin, Elin, and Florence exchange looks of satisfaction.*] I could imagine having a conversation with a colleague where I commended her for doing one of these well, or held her accountable for not doing enough of it. More importantly, I can see how more people doing more of these more of the time could really move the needle for Intrepid. How difficult was it to line up the leadership team on them—and how are you encouraging them, at that level? From what you told me in our first meeting, Alex, I can imagine that the last one especially, about open communication, has gotten a lot of attention.

[*The team members look to Alex to speak, but he gestures to Elin.*]

ELIN: I've asked the leaders to all make personal commitments to hold each other accountable for these behaviors. Once a month, in the leadership team meeting, we ask each leader to arrive with at least two specific examples—one where they have acted on a behavior and another where they've observed a behavior in action. We've opened each meeting by sharing these—it's been a good way to keep this culture dialogue alive and moving, through real specifics.

KATZ: That's a terrific example. And closer to the front line? I'm imagining that's what the great story is that I interrupted by walking in.

[*They all laugh.*]

FLORENCE: How did you know that, Katz?

KATZ: Because the most interesting and varied examples of how behaviors are changing are almost always down in the trenches where the real work gets done. So, what's happening in the trenches at Intrepid?

CALVIN: Well, we've brought back the green initiative, and this time we asked stores to opt in, rather than mandating it for everyone.

KATZ: [*Looking at Alex*] I think you've gone down this road before? With a green initiative?

FLORENCE: If you'll excuse me—I know what you're thinking, Katz. This isn't something top-down at all, like Toby's campaign. The idea came from frontline employees who had been—per our behaviors—listening to what the customers had to say. Customers had mentioned that a company's footprint influenced their buying decisions. So we've given stores that are interested the leeway to come up with and implement their own initiatives, and it's developed into a contest.

KATZ: So what's the great story?

CALVIN: One of our stores set up a table next to the checkout with scissors and a recycling bin, so customers can undo the packaging on their purchases for us to recycle. A few customers asked offhand questions like "What does this actually do?" and "What can you actually recycle this packaging into?" so one of the store associates set up a weigh station in the back of the store, then put up a large poster board showing how many pounds of packaging the store has recycled each week, as well as pictures of the things that could be made with the castoffs. The poster gets updated each week, and some of the pictures have been pretty hilarious. [*Turns his phone toward Katz*] Here's the one that had us all laughing.

KATZ: Who *are* those guys?

CALVIN: The store manager, Jess, and a customer, Callen— they mummified each other in bubble wrap!

KATZ: That's a great picture—and a really good story.

CALVIN: It's even better. The store now recycles about three times as much stuff as the average store. The employees in the back, even out of the customers' eyes, have become more conscious about whether packing materials end up in recycling or trash. And Jess, who was initially skeptical about the idea, has been thrilled with the community response and high customer engagement. She's going to take the idea to the summit next month for all the managers in her region; we're helping her with her presentation—that's why she sent this photo. Callen, the customer, is really involved in recycling initiatives in the community, so he shared a lot of ideas too. Ideally the regional leadership could then help the idea spread all across the company. We'll see. [*Looks at his watch*] Actually, we're checking in with her in a few. We should go. Great to see you, Katz.

[*Everyone leaves except Alex and Katz.*]

KATZ: Seems like a lot of good news and positive energy. How is business overall? And of course, I'm curious about the rumors we discussed on my last visit. I've been watching the news, and things still seem to be quiet on that front.

ALEX: I'm glad we have a chance to talk in private. I've been meaning to give you a call and fill you in. I sat down with the CEO of the startup, then went on a walk through their offices. The short version of the story is, I could just feel in my bones that this would not have been a culture fit. They are innovative and fast moving, and we'd love to bring those qualities into Intrepid. But they were also throwing money around—and a little full of themselves. I could not see our leadership team tolerating that. For now, it seems, Intrepid will stay the course as its own company.

KATZ: You must be relieved—and a little let down.

ALEX: Yes, that's right, a little of both. This whole emotional piece of leadership—it's complicated! It was a lot easier to just make rational decisions and not actually talk about how people *feel* about them. [*They both laugh.*]

KATZ: [*Smiling*] So now you're talking about emotions. I'm going to hazard a guess: you took my advice and you've been listening to your AILs.

ALEX: You guessed right. This initiative has been all about emotional energy. It's amazing how, when you try to get really precise and specific about intangible things like how people behave, you can unleash such a strong emotional response.

KATZ: Tell me more.

ALEX: Well, this green initiative of course is a great demonstration of the positive side of it. It's an idea that came out of regular meetings of our best authentic informal leaders, and the fact that it's actually taking flight is a huge source of pride for that group and a huge motivator to come up with even more new ideas. And we seem to be experiencing a slight uptick in overall profitability based mainly on reducing some costs; we need more time to get accurate data, but I suspect that running the stores in a greener way has a real benefit to the bottom line, as well as to consumer satisfaction and employee motivation.

KATZ: You should absolutely get that data. There is nothing like moving from "suspect" to "believe" to really give an initiative energy. People love to see that their actions are having impact and that that impact is good for the company's bottom line. And leaders, of course, are far more likely to keep supporting it over time.

ALEX: Great idea. [*Jots down a note*] There's a darker side to this, too. Once you give people a chance to open up, you have to really be willing to hear all their frustrations as well.

KATZ: Naturally. What is it that surprises you about what you're hearing? What are the sources of anger, sadness, and frustration in this company?

ALEX: I'm not sure it actually surprised me, but people at all levels of the business are well aware of how precarious the retail business is and what a threat this represents to Intrepid—today and in the future. Even with the recent gains, we are going to have to close some stores and lay off some good people—there is no way around it. As painful as that is, we've put it in motion.

KATZ: There are ways to put those kind of cost-containment efforts in motion that can respect people's emotions and help them get on board—it's worth a longer conversation. Layoffs and bad news don't mean you don't focus on culture—in fact, they mean that it's even more important to understand what motivates people even in tough times.

ALEX: Also, we did another employee survey, which was disappointing as well. Forty-eight percent of respondents believe that the changes implemented by senior managers do not seriously consider input from lower-level employees. The top reason people resist change, according to the survey, is that they don't understand the change that they're asked to make and therefore can't support it. The positive message I take from that is that at least people are aware of some of the barriers, so we can begin to address them.

KATZ: It still sounds like more good news than bad, right?

ALEX: I hope so. But I bet that if you asked people, they'd say we're only improving things around the edges. We haven't really shown how all of this will result in us becoming a really different kind of retail merchant.

KATZ: Well, this is where the measurement piece is going to be absolutely crucial. There is no better way of encouraging momentum than showing people that things are already changing. It's more impactful to show significant change in a small subpopulation than to show a small change across the whole organization. Cultural evolution takes time, and when folks see that a small group has already reaped significant benefit, they become hopeful that their turn will come and are interested in being the next guinea pig.

ALEX: So you're saying I should focus on measuring change at the stores that have opted into the green initiative.

KATZ: Spot on. Think about that story Calvin just told me. Coming up with the idea for that initiative—and that poster board—took initiative, creativity, and passion. And they have already come up with a metric—the weekly weigh-in of pounds of materials recycled in each store. I suspect they could come up with a few others— a simple one like per-store sales and maybe something else, like how likely a new customer is to return. What's important isn't that you find a perfect metric but that you stick with it consistently and encourage other stores to adopt it and do the same. I suggest you'll all find much to be encouraged about.

ALEX: That makes sense. Make the effort to connect *this* successful experiment to something broader.

KATZ: Exactly. Evolution is not a one-step process but an ongoing one. Elin's impulse to hold the leadership team mutually accountable for behavior change? Institution- alize it. Keep it on the agenda at the leadership team, and then encourage each member to implement it with direct reports, as well. Stories like the one I just heard? Keep sharing them. Those metrics from the green initia- tive pilot, like weighing the trash and recycling at the end of each week? Make them ongoing key performance indicators. And just keep looking.

ALEX: This really is a never-ending undertaking.

KATZ: Yes. As long as you're CEO, you'll never take your hand off the tiller of strategy and operations. You will need to stay responsive to the competition, to market shifts. Culture is just as dynamic and just as important. It's something you can't change overnight. But you can shape, align, and steer it—today, tomorrow, and for the long haul.

ALEX: I get that now. And I'm glad I have you to give me advice on this.

KATZ: I'm flattered, but you're wrong. I can tell, just by walking in the room today, that you're doing what you need to do—building an active council of foot soldiers who are on this journey with you.

THE IMPORTANCE OF MEASUREMENT

We hear two questions over and over from leaders as they digest and respond to the theory of the critical few. The first is, "How do I actually get people to act differently?" And the second is, "How will I know if my culture is improving?"

The answers to these questions are deeply intertwined. Helping your culture evolve is indeed possible. A culture evolution program does not consist of just talking and listening—once you identify the critical few traits, behaviors, and people, there are tangible actions that can shift a culture toward better alignment with your organization's purpose. One of the central messages of this book is that cultural situations evolve slowly over time. You can't point your finger and mandate behavior change. But you can intervene to create the conditions that make the right behaviors emerge. That's why we use the word *intervention* throughout this chapter as a broad term for any deliberate act that an organization undertakes to explain, encourage, reinforce, or reward critical behaviors. You're looking to surround your people with a coherent system of "enablers," some formal and some informal, that all, taken together, suggest a new path.

Interventions can take many forms, and this chapter outlines some ideas for how to design ones that will work for you and your people. The most effective interventions have three characteristics. First, they evolve out of the critical few behaviors discussions, and therefore they are, innately and by design, coherent with the overall message about how the desired behaviors will support the business. Second, they track and measure the tangible impact of putting the new behaviors into action—and, ideally, even attach these new ways of behaving to "hard" business results. Third, they appeal to the minds and hearts of those impacted.

Just as AILs are distinct from cultural ambassadors and change champions, behavior interventions are distinct from the top-down communications programs that accompany traditional transformation programs—the type that tend to result in colorful posters and wallet cards. Clear, top-down communications have a useful function in any organizational transformation. When well executed with clarity, consistency, and emotional commitment, communications send a strong message about future direction, expectations for people, and support from and alignment at the top. Communications alone are unlikely, however, to actually change the way that people work together. Katz likes to tell leaders, "I'm not worried about what you will say; I know you'll say all the right things. I'm more interested in what you will do." To move from a communications-led transformation to a true culture-led, behavior-focused transformation demands an approach that requires much more active engagement from people than simply downloading the latest FAQ. Interventions, when well designed, aim for the front line, where work gets done. They rewire how people work together day to day.

In this area, as in the area of selecting traits, behaviors, and informal leaders, the key to interventions and measurement is to focus on a critical few. You select a few targeted areas of your organization where a shift toward the identified behaviors—more people doing more of them more of the time—is most likely to have a tangible impact that can be seen and felt in a manner that helps people rally behind your cause. Working with your AILs, you codesign interventions that will help embed and reinforce the behaviors. Specific ideas will bubble up, as in, "Hey, we could all do more of behavior X by setting up a work group and meeting once a week to share ideas." We call these ideas "mechanisms" or "spreading mechanisms"—tangible ways that the behaviors can be put into practice. And you both measure and celebrate achievements often as you go, creating a self-perpetuating loop of reinforcement.

The only way to keep the momentum is for progress to be both made visible and acknowledged—it encourages and inspires others, and thus the critical behaviors are rewarded and repeated. To put it simply, this is why churches track funds raised for the church fair with plywood thermometers on the lawn and why online fundraising campaigns show progress toward a goal on their home page. It is encouraging simply to see progress, and that encouragement then helps the behaviors be repeated.

Why not start with your whole organization at once? Alternatively, why not begin with the leaders and then work your way down the organization layer by layer? Early interventions provide valuable learnings on what works well for your organization and highlight where appropriate customization will be useful. Top-down cascades, by definition, fail to solicit frontline input early on, so they miss the opportunity for energy and ideas from lower levels.

Furthermore, if you try to take on whole layers of the organization at once, you rely on everyone in that layer to be ready and willing at the exact same moment—a tall order! It's much easier to join forces with a few top executives who are excited to champion the cause, rope in a couple of managers who are similarly energized by driving behavioral change, and invite AILs who already exemplify the chosen critical behaviors. Just by pulling this group together, you're already halfway there. You are leveraging hierarchy and organizational support, involving middle management, and engaging the front line—all at the same time. You're focusing not on what's broken in your culture but on the pockets of positive energy—encouraging them to replicate and thrive. You can get to tangible results quickly and send a strong message to the organization that purposeful alignment of culture and strategy is of benefit to the whole enterprise.

This, of course, has to be seen to be believed—and so the rest of this chapter is dedicated to sharing ideas we've learned from our research and experience, using examples of organizations that have seen impressive results. The examples vary, but they have common themes. Leaders and AILs worked together to develop practical, let's-start-tomorrow ways of weaving new behaviors into the fabric of how work got done in their company. They conducted "pilots," a term we'll use throughout this chapter.

Pilots are deliberate experiments with new behaviors, real-time laboratories designed to highlight and acknowledge new ways of acting and attach these actions to measurable results. Pilots begin at a small scale and then, if effective, scale into broader programs or reforms. Pilot results demonstrate impact, build momentum, and serve as a proof of concept that this "soft stuff" really works. This chapter describes several examples from our work—pilot programs that were thoughtfully constructed, designed to attach the organization's "critical few" behaviors to meaningful results for the organization's business. In each of these examples, the set of metrics that moved—the scorecard for each of these efforts, in other words—was cocreated by the culture program leaders and the participants themselves. This cocreation has motivational benefits because people are far more energized by metrics that they have helped develop. And in each example, the scorecard is unique to that organization and its specific context.

We mention this here to forecast what might be a disappointment as you get to the end of the chapter: you will not find a "universal scorecard" exhibit that we have applied at one thousand other companies that you can pull out and use for your own organization. Hopefully, however, by the time you reach the conclusion of this chapter, you'll be persuaded by what's become vividly clear to us as we've explored these ideas through real client situations: the best way to make a real difference in your culture is by focusing on your own company's critical few behaviors, engaging your organization's authentic informal leaders, and developing your own company's specific, measurable approach to intervention. This is the secret to real, lasting culture evolution.

ASPIRATIONAL AND MEASURABLE GOALS

In 1987, Alcoa, the Aluminum Company of America, hired a new CEO, Paul O'Neill. O'Neill opened his first meeting with analysts and investors with a bold declaration: he would make worker safety his highest priority. Although analysts thought this was a bad decision and advised their clients to sell, O'Neill proved them all wrong. By the end of O'Neill's first year at the helm, profits at Alcoa had reached a record high, and by the end of his thirteen-year tenure, the company's performance had exceeded all expectations. And true to his promise, Alcoa became one of the safest companies in the world.

The transformation of Alcoa under O'Neill is a popular tale because it illustrates many appealing, counterintuitive points about management and leadership. It's an excellent example, of course, of how compassionate, employee-focused leadership can drive financial performance. Lives were saved, as well as dollars. When Katz conducted research at General Motors in the early 1990s, one plant manager credited O'Neill's safety notion with his entire plant turnaround simply because it gave him a tangible way to demonstrate to workers that he cared for them on a basic, human level. It's also a good keystone behavior story and is cited as such in *The Power of Habit* by Charles Duhigg. O'Neill, Duhigg writes, believed that some habits have the power to "start a chain reaction, changing other habits as they move through an organization."

The Alcoa safety example also illustrates how effective it can be to catalyze a comprehensive transformation through relentless focus on one aspirational, internal, measurable goal. Consider how different the goal "eliminate worker injury" is from more common organization-wide CEO mandates, like "beat competitors" or "be the best in the business." As opposed to these more general goals, "eliminate worker injury" demands that every single person in the business think consciously about how his or her own behaviors contribute. In this manner, it reminds us of one of our comprehensive culture evolution programs, conducted a handful of years ago at a technology client. The technology company was in the midst of a large-scale transformation. Our work focused on selecting critical behaviors and identifying and mobilizing a global cadre of authentic informal leaders. It also involved a deep-dive effort to focus on the customer experience and quality in one specific area: the quality of laptops within the personal computer business.

The company's leadership team had chosen to narrow in on laptop quality for its symbolic value. Internally and externally, it had been a red flag for several years running. Consumers complained about breakage and design flaws, both directly to customer service and in online forums. They sent back their laptops and demanded new ones—fair practice under the warranties and also very costly for the company. Analysis along the whole value chain of each laptop's development revealed many potential areas for improvement, such as product development processes and supplier management. Metrics related to these gap areas were limited. From the outside, it was difficult to dive in and see how to make a difference. Even where metrics were available, they were lagging instead of leading indicators and did not connect to performance ratings. In addition to these formal issues, the team discovered several informal areas for improvement, including poor communication across silos and insufficient working norms and behaviors. For example, people tended to create paperwork reporting on the issue instead of fixing problems.

Working with the business area leaders, the culture leadership established a comprehensive improvement program, including the traditional guardrails: redesigned metrics and incentives, improved development and handover processes. These guardrails were codesigned with the AILs in intense, hands-on, facilitated work sessions. These sessions also served as opportunities for the AILs to discuss and react to the critical behaviors and to talk about how these could or should be put into action to drive quality. At one point, to synthesize the ideas the AILs had offered, a facilitator drew an ideal new value chain on the whiteboard. The room went quiet. The facilitator paused the session and called attention to the discernible drop in energy and enthusiasm. She asked, "What, if anything, is stopping you today from putting these behaviors and this value chain into practice tomorrow?"

One manager raised his hand. "It's all well and good to look at the whole value chain," he said. "But the only thing I'm measured on is time to ship." It was a pin-drop moment: the truth had been spoken. The leaders had not discovered this incentive misalignment through their top-down gap analysis—it took someone who worked near the front line and handled the laptops every day to see and diagnose the problem. If the only metric that anyone paid attention to incentivized frontline workers to toss laptops into boxes in any condition, how and why would anyone focus on quality and the condition of the product in addition to speed of production?

But this isn't a simple story about how one tiny misaligned incentive can lead to dramatic unforeseen consequences, like the proverbial missing nail in the horse's shoe. This was a watershed in the company's overall culture evolution. The misalignment between the existing incentive and the goal of improving quality that the manager's comment brought to light was, of course, corrected. In addition, the entire set of metrics across the life cycle of products was redesigned. Prior to this program, every employee was, to some degree, measured on return rates that seemed both vague and after the fact. In other words, the metrics were not granular enough for any individual person to see that his or her own work had an impact on them; furthermore, the metrics all lagged, meaning they were tallied too late for any adjustments to be made in real time to alter them. Our overall effort involved establishing a much larger set of metrics that were designed to drive individual accountability in specific areas and balanced the leading and lagging indicators.

Without the culture program, this manager and other AILs would not have ever been in a forum that encouraged them to speak their mind so frankly. (And just as likely, the leaders would not have been primed to listen to it—and act on it.) The issue would have stayed under the radar of management, and as such would have contributed to foment skepticism at the front line relative to whether leaders were taking "quality" seriously. All the traditional, formal ways of trying to fix the quality program would likely have come up short.

Further, the AILs in the room who witnessed this moment and then saw leaders follow through and change the incentive experienced a powerful realignment of their expectations around leadership. They realized that their opinions mattered and their voices would be heard. They repeated the story outside the room. The story merged with and amplified a broader conversation taking place across the company about how things were different, things were improving. This small incident mattered because it took place as part of a larger movement and was consistent with that movement, was indeed representative of what the movement overall was trying to accomplish. Through repetition, the meaning of the story was reinforced. It acquired powerful emotional impact.

Within months, more than one thousand engineers had gone through quality behavior workshops. In addition, new metrics were introduced to evaluate the readiness of a product to move from one development phase to the next. Through these metrics, several hundred managers and frontline employees were now accountable for highly granular quality performance data. And crucially, they understood the behaviors required of them, as individuals and teams, to help them meet these marks and viewed this as a piece with the broader effect to transform the company.

Senior leaders also played a part: In both their day-to-day decision-making and their broader communications, they became much more explicit and direct about quality as a priority. The senior vice president of supply chain management set aside a full day each month for video conferences with all the suppliers and manufacturing partners to review Excel files detailing any issues with each product and resolve them line by line—a powerful symbolic act that demonstrated to both internal employees and external partners that the senior leadership was dedicated to problem solving and getting to the bottom of issues. Holding back a product to fix quality issues became an action to be proud of, not something for which to be blamed. And product managers loved it when their products were taken apart and examined—their work became a source of pride. Not surprisingly, the bottom-line result was an 8 percent improvement in warranty cost in year one of implementing the program, saving the company close to $100 million.

Another valuable point about interventions and measurement emerges from this example. Previous examples demonstrated how leadership's focus on a single metric— worker safety in Alcoa's case, laptop quality in the case of the tech company—can provide a focus and goal for a culture effort, catalyzing, as Duhigg notes, a "chain reaction" of further improvements. It's also worth pointing out, however, that the culture evolution team at the technology company did not focus solely on quality improvement—it was an aspirational metric that they hoped to see move, but it was also part of a broader ecosystem, a comprehensive program in which many elements overlapped and reinforced one another. Leaders walked the floor and openly acknowledged employees who demonstrated new behaviors. Some of these elements could, of course, not be measured. But some elements—such as the gradual increase in volunteer participants in the pride-builder program and the numbers of people who showed up for town halls—could be, and were, measured along the way. The overall approach taken at the technology company placed a premium on measurement, and this helped leaders constantly reinforce the core messages, track projects, and encourage forward momentum across the enterprise.

PILOTS: BRINGING BEHAVIORS INTO THE BUSINESS

Choosing the business issue or aspirational metric on which you will focus your interventions is important. It's also crucial to choose the area in your business—be it a department, facility, or function—that would be most opportune for the first pilots.

A combination of factors should play a role in this decision. You want to show the rest of the organization that when more people exhibit more of the critical few behaviors more of the time, good things happen—for them and for the organization's performance. So, start by looking for those executive and department leaders who support you, who are clearly energized by the topic of behavior-led transformation. Then, from this group, filter down to those who lead a manageable, midrange area of the business. If your initial group is too large or complex, it might be difficult to tackle right away. It also might take much longer to generate results. Small groups or very specialized groups also aren't ideal, though, because even groundbreaking results might not be recognized as applicable to the rest of the organization. And finally, filter out those groups that are dealing with a heavy burden. Trying to institutionalize a new set of behaviors in a refinery that's knee-deep in an ongoing maintenance turnaround is next to impossible. Similarly, avoid an IT function in the months running up to a major systems launch or a customer call center just as a major new product or promotion is being prepared for release.

Certainly, all these situations would benefit from more people acting out the critical few behaviors. (And be prepared—someone who owns one of these problems might argue vociferously for the special attention of being in the pilot because he or she wants to achieve a particular goal.) But in choosing one of them, you will risk not having the full attention of management and employees in that area because they will be more focused on their immediate goal than on the longer-term work of evolving behaviors. Also, if that group makes a huge leap in performance while focusing on behaviors, your results will be clouded by the other changes related to the ongoing process improvement. Think like a scientist conducting an experiment when selecting your pilot area: you want to be able to pinpoint areas of improvement and have it be crystal clear that implementation of the behaviors has made a difference. These areas will be the origins of the data you boast about, the stories that get told over and over—the formal and informal ways that anything gets rewarded.

But what if your entire organization is undergoing transformation—does that mean that the critical few approach can't work? Quite the contrary. If you are conducting an across-the-board transformation of your organization (or even a broad department within your organization), a critical few effort can be a powerful accelerant. Positive results and win stories travel quickly and can lead more people to jump on board.

An excellent illustration of this is the culture evolution we recently supported at a global agrochemical and agricultural biotech organization. The head of supply chain was leading an organization-wide manufacturing transformation, identifying areas of process improvement and applying lean manufacturing principles across all the production facilities. Wisely, he recognized that a real transformation required not only a comprehensive approach that included process improvements and lean practices but behavior changes as well. In our work, we focused on understanding each site's culture and the leadership behaviors required to support, enable, and drive these manufacturing aspirations. We facilitated discussions with frontline employees framed by two questions: "What are the strengths to build on?" and "What is stopping us from being great?" From these discussions, we came to understand when the customary ways of behaving were coming into conflict with the behaviors that would be necessary for all the other changes to stick.

This rich employee feedback supported the development of a critical few behaviors for each site. These behaviors were designed to reinforce the cultural strengths, thus encouraging positive emotions, and to address the most prominent pain points, thus reducing the potential for negative emotion.

The operating premise here was simple: positive emotions would encourage increased productivity. The behaviors were very specific and tangible; for example, "Promote transparency by increasing my availability on the floor and maintaining an open door protocol to address concerns and answer questions." Then, for each behavior, a culture team that included site leaders and human resource partners developed ideas (called "formal and informal enablers") that would help and support this behavior. These enablers ranged from tangible ideas that would be easy to execute (such as putting a suggestion box beside a manager's door) to complex proposals that would require concerted efforts across many stakeholders (such as significantly improving the documentation of all processes).

Next, for each of these ideas, we developed a charter proposing a series of steps for site leadership to put the idea into practice, including metrics by which leaders could trace progress in this area. (For an example of one of these charters, "Share Feedback and Coaching," see exhibit 5.1.) The program owner then presented these charters to senior leaders at a meeting convened to update them on the culture program to date and encourage them to select a "critical few" from a long list of behaviors. As the leaders discussed the portfolio of behaviors, they focused on the metrics; it was clear to them that they should select a few behaviors that could be documented and measured with relative ease. In other words, when it came to mechanisms for changing behaviors, measurability was a deciding factor in choosing the critical few.

MEASUREMENT AS AN APPROACH, NOT JUST AN OUTCOME

The agrochemical and agricultural biotech organization example—specifically, the charter the company designed for each mechanism—illustrates a useful point. As the culture team and the AILs worked together to design practical mechanisms that would encourage more people to exhibit each critical behavior more often, they kept asking the question, "And how would that be measured?" This perspective of perpetual inquiry helped them develop a nuanced, multifaceted approach with a lot of reassuring, solid metrics to report along the way. They were focused not just on one final big-

Critical Behavior Charter: Share Feedback and Coaching

Objectives

• Train and coach employees to effectively deliver and receive feedback

• Provide ad hoc coaching to help Site Leadership coach rather than teach others through the adoption of leadership behaviors

---

Context (historical performance, issues)

• Some employees do not feel comfortable providing feedback in complex situations

• Others do not feel coached through correcting and learning from mistakes

---

Key Stakeholders

• Site Leadership

• Human Resources for each site

• Change Management for each site

Benefit to Be Realized

• Boost organizational performance by helping individual employees work smarter, strengthen their skill set, and drive the adoption of desired behaviors

---

Metrics

• % employees provided regular on-the-job real-time feedback and coaching through setbacks

• % employees feeling able to provide negative feedback

• % employees feeling they have the tools and support to take on new challenges

• % employees feeling that Site Leadership holds employees accountable for their behaviors and work results

---

Exhibit 5.1 Example of "mechanism" charter from a critical few project

picture score, like worker safety at Alcoa or laptop quality at the technology company, but on a whole portfolio of leading indicators designed specifically to help build accountability and follow-through. Ultimately, your goal should always be to find a way to attach new behaviors to improved business results, even if that link can seem tenuous or indirect. The continuous effort to find that link, to make it real and tangible for others, should be your north star.

Just as with any other initiative or program, there are always opportunities to capture valuable data on effectiveness along the way. You can—and should—trace practical, tangible, simple information, like the number of people involved, responses received to email communications that are sent out related to the overall culture effort, and traffic to intranet sites that promote critical behaviors. This will help provide a baseline reference data set, allowing you to trace how momentum builds over time. Also look for data your organization is already capturing, such as employee engagement scores, and track whether any of these scores rise. This is especially effective if you preselect, early on, specific questions that relate to behavior areas where you are trying to make a difference—for example, if you have a critical behavior related to empowering employees at all levels, you might narrow in on a specific engagement survey question, such as the response rate to "I feel encouraged to come up with new and better ways of doing things." You could even break out this data by level and investigate how the rate changes over time or by area of the business and assess whether any pilots improved those scores.

It's also possible to build new data capture tools, such as behavior pulse surveys, an example of which is shown in exhibit 5.2. These surveys are, by design, quick and easy to respond to and ask only about the employees' opinion on whether the desired behaviors are showing up in the organization. In chapter 4, we described the organizational network analysis rolled out across a bank to locate its exemplars and influencers. That survey also incorporated a pulse survey on the key behaviors to set a baseline. Leaders in this company intend to continue to employ this behavioral pulse check as an ongoing key performance indicator (KPI) to capture the momentum of their movement and identify areas where the behaviors are "taking" versus those where progress is not being made. This will help the leaders understand how and where to direct future interventions.

For the four questions below, please select an answer from 1 (Strongly Disagree) to 10 (Strongly Agree). We would like you to share with us the degree to which the following behaviors are happening in your current working environment.

- Leaders at all levels help **connect my work to the larger purpose of serving our customers with integrity.**
- Leaders and colleagues at all levels **work with other areas to create common goals and follow through urgently.**
- Leaders at all levels **enable me to take ownership of my work and help remove obstacles that arise.**
- The three behaviors (**mentioned in bold** above) are positively impacting our business performance today.

Exhibit 5.2 Example of a pulse survey

Finally, pay attention to stories that emerge along the way. Often, when an organization is successfully evolving its culture, stories about new ways of behaving that demonstrate "it's not just business as usual around here" pop up and go viral. An incident becomes a story that others repeat because it contains some powerful truth —an implicit lesson that resonates with other experiences and conversations. The technology company story of the manager speaking his mind about metrics is, of course, a great example. When this kind of story emerges, grab it and make use of it—if people already find it interesting enough to pass it around, do what you can to amplify its impact. Mention it in communications, call out the "stars" of the story publicly, and ask them to speak more about their experience. But don't just wait for stories to emerge: actively cultivate them by encouraging people to frame their experiences of witnessing how behaviors are evolving in story form.

Some companies make storytelling a standing agenda item for the groups of AILs. This helps focus discussions on clear articulations of what a behavior looks like in the work that gets done in the company every day. You can also solicit stories more broadly, and even make storytelling a theme of your entire culture evolution; we've seen some organizations run CEO-sponsored contests for best behavior story, hold TED talk–style meetings where frontline leaders tell stories to broad audiences of how things are changing, and conduct storytelling training as a form of intervention. These are all excellent ideas, and I also encourage you to remember that these stories are also a data set—you should be disciplined about collecting them along the way, analyze them to make their meanings clear, and report on their numbers and emergence just as you would with other "harder" metrics.

James served an energy company in the Middle East on a culture transformation project that was nearly two years in duration. Over the course of this project, he got to know a particular manager. This manager began as a great skeptic, but over the course of their collaboration he came to be a strong believer in what they called, on that project, "behavior-based transformation." At one point in the program, he was asked to report results to senior leaders. This is a direct quote from his enthusiastic report:

> If I were to tell you that in six months we went from having ten people in my organization talking about and making commitments to our critical few behaviors to one hundred, *and* that the whole of my organization has gone from reporting us as a five-out-of-ten in terms of the prevalence of these behaviors to a seven, *and* we have a dozen positive anecdotes about things happening that weren't previously observed, *and plant availability* (the business KPI that we cited as a priority before we started) has improved by 5 percent—*then* would you believe me when I say that I think we're making good progress?

We love this quote! It illustrates the core point of this chapter about measurement and impact—that it is complex, multifaceted, and possible. The combination of measures expressed in this statement is very powerful. It pulls in aspects of participation (going from ten to one hundred people), custom-designed behavior survey results (going from a five-out-of-ten to a seven), and close observation of emerging stories of the behaviors in action (having a dozen positive anecdotes). Finally, it makes an explicit link to the business outcomes (improving plant availability by 5 percent). While the manager does not explicitly connect that 5 percent improvement in the tracked KPI to the critical behaviors, it is clear that he sees and believes in a causal correlation between them.

MEASUREMENT IS EMOTIONAL

James has worked with a mining company in the Middle East with mines and processing facilities that extend across the region. The organization's workforce represents an extraordinary cross section of ethnicities, religious backgrounds, and even languages. The culture evolution program that James and the company's leaders designed was, for those leaders, an important opportunity to ensure that the organization's values were understood all across the company, as well as to align organization-wide behaviors with the strategic goal of continued geographic expansion.

This company, like the banking firm described in chapter 4, used a network analysis to identify the AILs and then gathered these authentic leaders for full-day facilitated workshops to discuss the critical behaviors, how they might be embedded at all levels in the day-to-day work, and what some potential metrics might be for tracking and demonstrating their manifestations. One critical behavior was demonstrating respect for others and for their workspace. At one processing facility, the AILs posited that safety and cleanliness of the physical locations where work got done was an accurate reflection of people's respect for one another. The heavy metals industry in general and the facilities where metals are processed specifically require dirty, dangerous work; to the people who work at these locations every day, the links between cleanliness, safety, and respect are not abstract but direct. Together with the culture program leaders, the AILs identified a list of mechanisms that would encourage individuals to take personal responsibility for the collective cleanliness and safety of each site. They also developed an interesting metric for this behavior: waste management.

In several interviews and dialogues, AILs noted how dispiriting and frustrating it was to take waste out to the trash bins and notice that others hadn't bothered to dispose of their own waste according to regulations but had simply left it beside the bins. This spoke to them of lack of respect; people were, when alone, behaving in ways that did not consider the impact that their actions had on others. One AIL proposed that a photograph be taken each week of the bins' condition after a week of use before they were emptied. The photographs, week after week, documented progress from a site where people did not behave in ways that demonstrated their mutual respect for one another's safety to one where this behavior was embedded—where the ground beside the bin was bag-free and clean.

We love this example because the organization's leaders, as earnest and well-meaning as they were, never could have developed this mechanism and related metric. (Recall that we made this same point about the discovery of the misaligned quality metric in the technology company story earlier in this chapter. Let us underline this message here: listen to your AILs!) One must work at that facility to understand the actual and emotional impact that the sight of those trash bins had on the people whose job it was to navigate around them—and what this communicated about the lack of respect for others. The photographs, over time, served as a measure of progress. And the fact that the leaders studied them and took them seriously was progress of a different sort—the evolution of a very hierarchical organization toward one where leaders were actively, deliberately learning to consider the perspectives of people who did the tough work of their industry every day.

LOOKING AHEAD AT CULTURE AND MEASUREMENT

We will be the first to admit it: culture is a "fuzzy" topic, one for which establishing firm rules or universal standards of measurement is difficult. Our aim has been to convince you, with the stories and examples we've shared, that it is indeed possible to move conversations about culture from the theoretical toward the empirical. The key is to be practical and disciplined and to listen very hard to the voices of the people who do real work. You want to choose metrics just like you choose behaviors—not according to some abstract set of ideals but by paying close attention to the way real work gets done and what matters emotionally to people.

The longer we spend in this culture game, the more aware we become that this is an area of study still in its infancy. Other practitioners in this space are searching for or claim to have created a reliable, universal index that can measure whether a culture is "working." We encourage these efforts and hope to someday applaud and embrace one as successful. For now, though, we will continue to encourage clients—and to encourage you, the reader—to focus not on an abstract idea of what the "best" culture is but on what is strongest, most reliable, and most effective within your current culture. We believe that is the quickest and most effective way to get the best out of people.

In our work at the Katzenbach Center, we are one small part of a larger movement of theorists and practitioners who are looking to make advances in the study of the "softer side" of organizations. In 2016, Morgan Stanley published "A Framework for Gender Diversity in the Workplace," which proposed a correlation between companies that had made deliberate formal steps to address gender equity and stock returns and volatility related to those companies' financial performance. Using a quantitative model that incorporates not just the mix of women and men at different levels of the company but also factors such as pay equity, maternity leave policy, and the existence of flexible work opportunities, the researchers were able to create a score that ranks companies relative to what Morgan Stanley calls their "gender diversity culture" and then connect that score to their standard financial metrics, such as returns and volatility. Morgan Stanley's data is conclusive: "More gender diversity, particularly in corporate settings, can translate to increased productivity, greater innovation, better decision-making, and higher employee retention and satisfaction."

We end here with this study because we were so inspired by this effort to make a clear connection between measurable, quantifiable root causes and a broad "cultural/behavioral" issue, gender diversity. We believe that the curiosity of colleagues inside and outside our own networks and the forms of data that are now available to all of us will allow more studies like this to proliferate in years ahead, further clarifying the connections between how we all behave, feel, and operate at work and how our organizations perform. And we would like to challenge you, our reader, not to rush out and build a model like this for your own company but to take away the simple idea that measuring and quantifying aspects of a culture not only is possible but can lead to some powerful insights.

Epilogue

SCENE: Mid-December. One of Intrepid's retail stores. The store is bustling; it's a weekday afternoon in the midst of the holiday season.

ALEX: Thanks so much for taking the time to come and walk through this store with me. I know that everybody's lives are so busy, especially at this time of year.

SEBASTIAN: It's my pleasure. The whole board has been so interested to hear about your efforts related to culture. I jumped at an invitation to see it in action.

ALEX: I told the manager, Jess, that we'd be here, and she's excited to give us a walk-through of both the customer spot for the package removal and the improved recycling center in the back by the docks. She's in a staff meeting until noon. [*Checks his watch*] We're a little early: let's get a feel for the store.

[Sebastian and Alex are speaking in low tones and are dressed casually in jeans and sport shirts. It's clear that they don't want the store employees to feel that they're being "spied on" by management. They notice that a customer and an employee, an older woman and a young man, are embroiled in an intense conversation at the end of the aisle. The holiday music is loud, and their words are not discernible. The customer seems frustrated, but

the employee's face is calm; eventually, the woman's face and posture mirror that of the employee, more relaxed and open. The employee is writing something down. Both smile, and they part ways. The employee heads toward the front of the store, in the direction of Sebastian and Alex. Alex stops him.]

ALEX: Hey there—I want to introduce myself. I'm Alex, the CEO of Intrepid. I don't mean to embarrass you, but I came here today because I've been hearing from the management how well this store is doing and wanted to see it for myself. I just got lucky enough to watch you in action—you seemed to be solving a problem for that customer. What was going on?

DANIEL: [*A little flustered*] The CEO, seriously?

SEBASTIAN: [*Kindly, putting out his hand*] Yes, and he puts his pants on one leg at a time. I'm Sebastian, and your name is?

DANIEL: I'm Daniel—great to meet you both.

ALEX: So what was happening with that customer?

DANIEL: She wanted to return something she bought on-line without a receipt—said she has the box in the car but not the receipt that came with it. It's against policy, but I told her that I'd see what I can do. She's going to get what she has and meet me at the returns counter—I know the guys who work there, and I can talk to them. [*Looking concerned, suddenly aware he's talking to management*] Does that sound right to you guys?

ALEX: She walked away happy—I think it sounds like you listened to her and are trying to work with her. When a process doesn't work, we focus on how to make that process more flexible. And we respond to what the customers feel—that was clear to me, even from twenty feet away. You were well aware of what she was feeling, and it made a huge difference.

DANIEL: Thanks! That means a lot to hear. I should make sure I'm at returns when she gets there. It was great to meet you both. Thanks for saying hi. [*Heads toward the front of the store*]

SEBASTIAN: That was pretty impressive!

ALEX: [*With pride*] Yes, we have some great people. And the more I do this—come to the stores and local offices, walk the halls—the more I realize what a difference it can make. I just managed to talk about two of our critical behaviors, and it felt pretty natural. There's real value in repetition and consistency, in conveying messages until you think you are going to run out of breath, and applying them to the context at hand. This is definitely something I've learned in the past year.

SEBASTIAN: So how have you made this work? To what do you credit all these changes?

ALEX: Well, personally, I am learning how to delegate more and to empower my team. I ran a very intense program on culture and behaviors for all of this year directly out of my office. I'm moving it over to human resources now to become a part of our overall people processes. The employee who led it, Calvin, will become my chief of staff.

SEBASTIAN: That's great to hear.

ALEX: I've really come to see that a culture is operating effectively when everyone has the power to focus on themselves and asks what they can do to lead and that it all comes down to behaviors—repeated, consistent, clear behaviors. And those behaviors need to be motivated by the positive emotions that result. People need to feel good about doing what matters most. Now, I will put on overalls and clean up and pick up aisles if that's what I'm asking my people to focus on. I more often play the role of a tiebreaker than a speaker. I am meeting with suppliers again, which I have missed, and I write a blog about it so that it's visible to our employees. I respect my employees, understand them better, and feel like we're on the same team. When I go to an area, I ask the people what they've done to cut costs, and we enjoy the conversation about it. Our focus is good.

SEBASTIAN: How did it work? Give me a sense of the process.

ALEX: First, we set up three groups of twelve to fifteen of our best motivators in selected parts of our business, which took about six weeks. Next, we expanded by setting up nine additional motivator groups of twelve to fifteen across each key business area, which took us another eight weeks. Third, we focused on encouraging existing groups to expand and new groups to form to engage more people across the organization. Each group member set up his or her own group of ten to twenty extended members, which took another four months. Now, in our final stage, we allow groups to expand or contract organically. Sure, we facilitate connections between different groups to share learning and insights and continue to support and energize. But the change has occurred, and I feel increasingly pleased about where this all seems to be heading.

Importantly, we can feel the difference. Although there are some measurable results, a lot of the results are not measurable. We started by leveraging positive emotions to define our best culture and ended with emotion sustaining the culture. People keep saying that they have never had such a good time at work, even though they are working harder. We are inspired by the challenges ahead, where once we were afraid.

SEBASTIAN: I'm on the board of another organization that is facing issues very similar to the ones that we were talking about here a year ago—an industry in decline, an organization where people were struggling to find the motivation to stay the course. What advice would you give to their CEO?

ALEX: My strongest lesson has been learning to consider Intrepid's cultural situation with realism and pragmatism. I'm no longer obsessed with changing our culture. I see instead that most of it is beneath the surface, almost subliminal, the water we swim in, the air we breathe. And I look for ways to see its strength in action and to encourage the right behaviors by making people feel good about mastering those behaviors, as well as about the results they yield—just like I did now with Daniel. I notice when it's working, more than obsessing about when it's getting in the way. And I commit to shaping it over time, just like I do our strategic and operating priorities.

Culture is never all good or all bad. As long as we keep it a part of our focus, it will enable us to sustain our distinctiveness over time—whatever the future holds.

Appendix

A sample focus group agenda and interview questions are included here as illustration and support tools to guide you in your own cultural evolution journey.

Sample Focus Group Agenda

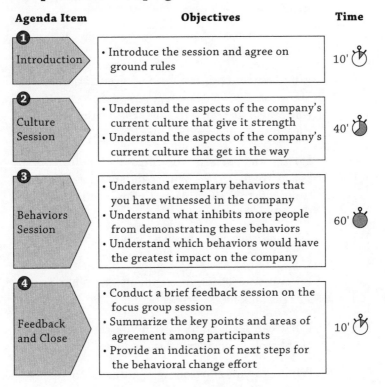

Agenda Item	Objectives	Time
1 Introduction	• Introduce the session and agree on ground rules	10'
2 Culture Session	• Understand the aspects of the company's current culture that give it strength • Understand the aspects of the company's current culture that get in the way	40'
3 Behaviors Session	• Understand exemplary behaviors that you have witnessed in the company • Understand what inhibits more people from demonstrating these behaviors • Understand which behaviors would have the greatest impact on the company	60'
4 Feedback and Close	• Conduct a brief feedback session on the focus group session • Summarize the key points and areas of agreement among participants • Provide an indication of next steps for the behavioral change effort	10'

Sample Culture Interview Questions

- How would you describe the culture of your organization?

  - What are some aspects of the culture that you feel are distinctive or unique (e.g., relationship based, metrics driven)? What makes people proud to work here?

- Can you describe any specific behaviors or aspects of the culture that detract from your strategic goals?

  - What keeps you up at night? What do you complain about at home?

- What elements of the formal organization (formal processes, rules, structure, etc.) get in the way of people trying to "live" the best of the culture in their day-to-day work?

- Do certain parts of the organization function better than others? What's different? What are some of the effective behaviors you observe there?

  - Which specific individuals display these effective behaviors?

- What is your vision for your culture? What does success look like?

- What can leadership start doing right away to visibly role-model your desired behaviors?

- What can you start doing right away to visibly role-model your desired behaviors?

Glossary of Key Terms

authentic informal leaders/AILs. People who influence and energize others without relying on their title or formal position in the hierarchy to do so. They have an innate ability to influence others and are a powerful resource to spread critical few behaviors from the bottom up.

behaviors. Patterns within a company of how individuals spend their time, make decisions, live relationships, handle conflicts and truths, and perform their jobs; what people "do" on a day-to-day basis.

critical few. A strategic, thoughtfully selected subset of traits, behaviors, people, or emotions, narrowed down for the purpose of having the most impact on a company within the shortest possible period of time.

cultural action/intervention. Targeted acts that alter and influence how people behave day to day; in some contexts, called "spreading mechanisms" or "enablers."

cultural boost. A burst of positive energy across the organization, a series of integrated moments when employees at all levels feel positive energy connections about their affiliation with the organization.

cultural coherence/incoherence. In the positive form, a state to be aspired to, where culture, strategy, and operating model all are in alignment. In the negative form, a state where it's discernible to people that a company's culture does not support its strategic goals.

cultural insight. Knowledge of how work "actually gets done" within an organization—what people feel strongly about, what motivates people; in this methodology, the self-knowledge that develops as a result of a thorough diagnostic.

culture. The self-sustaining patterns of behaving, feeling, thinking, and believing that determine how things are done within an organization.

culture thumbprint. A "critical few" unique, characteristic organizational traits, enriched by positive and negative behavioral manifestations; in this methodology, the output of a thorough diagnostic—the synthesis of the collective input of many members of an organization through focus groups, interviews, and sometimes a survey.

emotional energy. A collective response of people within an organization that is difficult to explain or recognize through a purely rational framework or set of reasons. Emotional energy always exists but usually becomes visible to leaders or outsiders when triggered by some stimulus—a crisis, a leadership announcement, a change in policy, a shift in strategic direction. Like a trait, it can have both positive and negative manifestations.

keystone behaviors. A term coined by Charles Duhigg for select behaviors that, if repeated over time, can help change habits. In this methodology, used to refer to behaviors that can be practiced organization-wide to help evolve a culture.

KPI. Key performance indicator used to measure the impact of behavior change.

leading outside the lines. An approach to management premised on the idea of harnessing/leveraging an organization's formal and informal sides, helping them "jump together." See Jon Katzenbach and Zia Khan's book by this title.

mechanisms or spreading mechanisms. An initiative to support the critical behaviors in a culture evolution effort; also, interventions.

neutral. In this methodology, an aspiration for descriptive traits of an organization, meant to designate that a trait has both positive and negative potential manifestations; significant because core to the premise that no culture has "good" or "bad" elements—that all traits can be understood as both enabling and interrupting strategic aspirations.

symbolic act. A deliberate, purposeful action taken by leadership that sends a strong archetypal message; a form of cultural intervention that is specific to those in a leadership role.

trait. A recognized organization-wide tendency for people to behave in a certain way. A trait's "neutrality" means that it has positive and negative repercussions, representing two sides of the same coin.

values. Fundamental beliefs of a person or organization that guide behavior and action, always positive and aspirational in nature.

Bibliography

This list does not aspire to provide a comprehensive overview of the field of writings on organizational culture. Instead, we have chosen to highlight some of the works (including, rather immodestly, Katz's own) that either are referenced in the text of *The Critical Few* or are most salient to the core concepts of our methodology. We hope you'll find these resources helpful.

Duhigg, Charles. *The Power of Habit: Why We Do What We Do in Life and Business*. New York: Random House, 2012.

Duhigg's best-selling book explores the science behind habit formation and how to use that knowledge to change habits. Duhigg's idea of "keystone habits" that can trigger other habits in individuals and their peers correlates to how powerful we believe the critical few behaviors can be to organization-wide transformations.

Goleman, Daniel. *Emotional Intelligence: Why It Can Matter More than IQ*. New York: Bantam Books, 1995.

Goleman's influential book discusses the importance of the emotional mind (versus the rational mind) in human interaction. He describes the five crucial components of emotional intelligence—self-awareness, self-regulation, internal motivation, empathy, and social skills—and how they can be learned. The focus of Katz's life work has been to harness sources of emotional energy within organizations to meet strategic goals.

Herzberg, Frederick. "One More Time: How Do You Motivate Employees?" *Harvard Business Review*, 1968. Reprint, *Harvard Business Review* (January 2003): 87–96.

Herzberg's article analyzes the differences between factors that lead to employee engagement and those that lead to dissatisfaction.

Herzberg was one of the first to argue that employee dissatisfaction cannot be addressed solely through "formal" factors such as company policy and compensation; motivation must stem from factors intrinsic to the work itself and recognition from others for achievement. What makes both a pride builder and an authentic informal leader is the ability to motivate others in the manner that Herzberg describes.

Katzenbach, Jon R. *Why Pride Matters More Than Money: The Power of the World's Greatest Motivational Force*. New York: Crown Business, 2003.

Every company has unique sources of pride, and uncovering these sources is a critical part of understanding the existing culture as well as selecting the right "critical behaviors" that drive performance. The idea of an emotion as the primary driver of human performance that Katz introduces in *Why Pride Matters* is fundamental to *The Critical Few*.

Katzenbach, Jon R., and Zia Khan. *Leading outside the Lines: How to Mobilize the Informal Organization, Energize Your Team, and Get Better Results*. New Jersey: Wiley, 2010.

The premise of this book—that the best companies manage a sort of ambidexterity that balances the "formal" and "informal"— echoes the idea in *The Critical Few* that emotional and rational forces within an organization must align for superior performance. The book posits the "informal organization" as the network of emerging ideas, social networks, working norms, values, peer relationships, and communities of common interest that drive how people behave.

Katzenbach, Jon R., and Douglas K. Smith. *The Wisdom of Teams: Creating the High-Performance Organization*. Boston: Harvard University Press, 1993.

Katz's first major book, rereleased in 2015, makes the core argument that there is no one ideal structure for teams. The strongest teams are those that can flexibly adapt their working styles in response to the challenges at hand. Katz now believes that this

early work, as influential as it has been, misses a central point—
that an individual team's capability reflects not just its members'
own choices but the ecosystem of the organizational culture that
surrounds them. However, *The Wisdom of Teams*' argument that
every team contains within it the ability to become "high perform-
ing" presages a fundamental idea in *The Critical Few*.

Katzenbach, Jon R., Ilona Steffen, and Caroline Kronley. "Cultural
Change That Sticks," *Harvard Business Review* (July–August 2012).
This article was early in making the point that if leaders want
to evolve their culture, it's better to work within that culture than
fight it. The authors point out that enterprises attaining peak
performance get there by applying five principles: match strategy
and culture, focus on a few critical shifts in behavior, honor the
strengths of your existing culture, integrate formal and informal
interventions, and measure and monitor cultural evolution. Such
companies see culture as a competitive advantage—an accelerator
of change, not an impediment.

Leinwand, Paul, and Cesare Mainardi, with Art Kleiner. *Strategy
That Works: How Winning Companies Close the Strategy-to-Execution
Gap*. Boston: Harvard Business Review Press, 2016.
Executives today often grapple with closing the gap between
strategy and execution. In *Strategy That Works*, the authors explore
common pitfalls and demonstrate how some of the best companies
in the world consistently outperform others. The notion of "cohe-
sion" between elements at the heart of this book is very similar
to the idea of the dynamic tension between strategy, operating
model, and culture that we posit in *The Critical Few*. The authors
argue that "putting your culture to work" is one of the five acts of
unconventional leadership common to the world's best companies.

Schein, Edgar. *Organizational Culture and Leadership*. New Jersey:
Jossey-Bass, 1985.
This classic is now in its fifth edition. Schein is considered the
father of organizational culture, and this book serves as a primer

on the topic. It discusses how cultures are formed, the role of culture in the management of organizational change, and the role of leadership in shaping and guiding culture. It is a foundational text for any reader interested in this topic.

Acknowledgments

In this book, we strive to bring simplicity and clarity to a very complicated topic. The origin story of this book, meanwhile, is anything but straightforward. If any book could claim to have many authors, it would be *The Critical Few*. The methodology at its heart evolved out of real work done by real people with real clients. The projects, relationships, and experiences that inspired the story of Alex and Intrepid have spanned three firms—the original Katzenbach Partners, founded in 1999; Strategy& (formerly Booz & Company), into which Katzenbach Partners integrated in 2008; and PwC, our current home after its acquisition of Strategy& in 2014. Along the way, many committed and brilliant thinkers and practitioners have placed their hands on this clay. We will do our best to name them all, and if you have been forgotten here in this document, know that we will someday remember, slap our collective foreheads, and beg for your forgiveness.

CORE PRACTITIONERS AND CONTRIBUTORS

The Strategy& Katzenbach Center at PwC has a small core team fully dedicated to running the center and a dedicated coterie of practitioners who actively "practice what we preach." Together, this core team and global leadership team (GLT), with the addition of a few other very dedicated individuals, constitute the Katzenbach Center Community of Practice, named collectively as coauthors. Among this community of practice, we owe an especial debt to DeAnne Aguirre, who, in addition to a host of other institutional responsibilities, is the Strategy& US/Mexico leader and the global sponsor of the Katzenbach Center within PwC. We are also indebted to Tim Ryan, US chairman and senior partner at PwC, and

Robert Moritz, PwC global chairman, for their ongoing support of this project and our work.

Here are a few memories of how this group came to be. From the Middle East, Per-Ola Karlsson has also served as a guiding voice to the center and played a leadership role in one of the most comprehensive multiyear culture evolution efforts we've had the pleasure to conduct—a project that also brought Roger Rabbat, another GLT member, into our fold. In Australia, Varya Davidson has been a tireless champion, building a local community of practice that includes Michelle Kam, Julian Ballard, and many others. From Europe, Frédéric Pirker, Diana Dimitrova, and Paolo Morley-Fletcher have been dedicated coleaders, and Paolo has been especially focused on integrating his deep passion for leadership development and coaching with this approach. Another leadership aficionado, Barry Vorster, has brought fascinating client situations from Africa into our repertoire. And in North America, the persistent efforts of Amanda Evison, Jaime Estupiñán, and Kristy Hull have lent this methodology a depth and resonance that would otherwise be absent—they are truly practitioners in every sense of the word.

For the past six years, the Katzenbach Center has run a fellows program through which talented, curious people in the first few years of their career in client service affiliate with us for a year to learn our methods. All our current and former fellows have contributed to our thinking in some way, such as AB Allam, Varun Bahatnagar, Simon Brown, Sean Buchholtz, Kevin Burke, Martin Crew, Jessica Geiger, Katie Griffith, Mike Neff, Tripp Fried, Vivian Pang, Alexander Pearlman, Hana Reznikov, Gideon Rutherford, Caroline Smit, Kirsten Verlander, Elena Weinstein, and Inshita Wij. We are also proud to note that a "critical few" then folded their careers, for a time, back into our core team and have made significant contributions to our work; we are lucky to count Kate Dugan, Alice Zhou, and Cindy Pan in this category. Other core team members include Brian Wayland, Katz's right hand and our team's operations center; Carolin Oelschlegel, whose move from Europe to the United States helped solidify the team's global perspective; and

Reid Carpenter, who also serves as the US leader of the Katzenbach Center and part of the global leadership team. Reid has been tireless in her advocacy and support of this project. In fact, without her selfless willingness to shoulder even more responsibility than usual, it is more than fair to say that there would be no book.

Within and across PwC, many individuals have offered us guidance and advice. We are grateful for the support and sponsorship of Paul Leinwand, Randy Browning, Deniz Caglar, Vinay Couto, Carrie Duarte, Miles Everson, Mohamed Kande, Joachim Rotering, and Carol Stubbings, as well as Bill Cobourn, Stephanie Hyde, Hilal Halaoui, Tom Puthiyamadam, Blair Sheppard, David Suarez, and John Sviokla. Special thanks to our HIA leaders who have provided an excellent home for the past several years: Kelly Barnes, Jeff Gitlin, Jae Kim, and Bob Glenn. The advice and counsel of Kanchi Bordick, Justine Brown, Daniel Garcia, Nadia Kubis, Matt Lieberman, Jennifer Myers, Martina Sangin, and Ilona Steffen have benefited us enormously.

We also have a broad global network of others who bring this work to clients and return to the center with new anecdotes, examples, and suggested changes to our methods. This group is too broad to fully articulate, but a few who have made a big contribution to our efforts are Peter Bertone, Antonia Cusamano, Henning Hagen, Matt Mani, Deniz Caglar, Matt Siegel, Matt Egol, Earl Simpkins, Carole Symonds, Kenji Mitsui, Jay Godla, Thom Bales, Patrick Maher, Igor Belokrinitsky, Sundar Subramanian, Rick Edmunds, Greg Rotz, and Surajit Sen. In addition, Murielle Tiambo, Maureen Trantham, Augusto Giacomman, Aaron Newman, and Sarah Nathan have all served as comrades in the field.

This book would not exist without the inspiration of Art Kleiner, editor-in-chief for PwC Global and its magazine *strategy+business*, who has shepherded us along from early days through our well-advised introduction to Berrett-Koehler. *Strategy+business* editors Dan Gross and Michelle Gerdes also provided guidance to the Katzenbach Center that indirectly benefited this book. Huge thanks also to the many PwC internal marketing and editorial partners who guided and supported us along the way: Susan Brown, Madeleine Buck, Mao-Lin Shen, Shannon King, L. Parker Barnum, Mike Manning, Jeffery McMillan, Dee Hildy, Molly Lang, Siobhan Ford, Jaime Dirr, Elizabeth Barrett, Ann-Denise Grech, Bevan Ruland, and Natasha Andre. Other writing and proofreading assistance that helped keep this project on track came from Michael Walker, who organized the material into our original outline; Faith Florer, who produced a first draft; and Victoria Beliveau, who copyedited the final draft.

Other Key Contributors

Others outside our firm have guided our thinking with real, deep insight. We continue to share ideas with former Katzenbach Partners colleagues, such as Niko Canner, Zia Khan, Shanti Nayak, John Rolander, Kerry Sulkcowicz, and Maggie van de Griend. An introduction to Charles Duhigg was serendipitous, as his "keystone behaviors" idea has proved so resonant with our own approach. Former Katzenbach Partners colleague Amy Gallo, now a writer and editor, has provided wise and generous counsel. We are all grateful to Chad Gomes, who has played a crucial contributor role by sharing many useful anecdotes and pearls of wisdom from his fieldwork on this topic and has separately been a friend and collaborator with each one of us. Our editors at Berrett-Koehler, Neil Maillet, Michael Crowley, and Jeevan Sivasubramaniam, have stunned us with their warmth and encouragement.

Over the years since the conversations about this book began, families—ours and those of our closest core team and collaborators—have supported us along the way. They have also evolved, as all institutions do: expanding, contracting, and taking new shapes. On the topic of expansion, our core Katzenbach Center team has proved particularly adept in the production of progeny, and we had fun naming the characters in the narrative after these much-adored children. Will the real Avery, Calvin, Callen, Casimir, Elin, Florence, Jane, Ross, Sebastian, and Theodore—all born since this project began—please take a bow?

Index

Page references followed by *e* indicate an exhibit.

About the Authors

Jon R. Katzenbach, James Thomas, and Gretchen Anderson are leaders at the Katzenbach Center, a global knowledge center focusing on culture and leadership at PwC's Strategy&. The center aims to unite like-minded individuals inside and outside the firm who are passionate and curious about the intersection of people, culture, and organizations. The Katzenbach Center builds capabilities related to its core content areas, conducts original research, provides coaching and support to teams, and works directly with clients. For access to our latest thinking, follow our blog series, *The Critical Few*, on *strategy+business* (https://www.strategy-business.com/the-critical-few).

Jon R. Katzenbach is the founder of the Katzenbach Center at Strategy&, PwC's strategy consulting business. With more than five decades of experience advising leaders, Jon is a recognized expert in organizational performance, collaboration, corporate governance, culture challenges, and employee motivation. Before the integration with PwC, Jon was a senior partner with Strategy& (formerly Booz & Company). Prior to Booz & Company, Jon was founder of Katzenbach Partners LLC, a firm specializing in organization, leadership, governance, and strategy. For thirty years prior to founding his own firm, he was a director with McKinsey. He is the author or coauthor of many articles and notable books, including *The Wisdom of Teams*, *Peak Performance*, *Leading outside the Lines*, and *Why Pride Matters More Than Money*. Articles published in recent years that presage ideas in this book include "10 Principles of Organizational Culture" in *strategy+business*, coauthored with James Thomas and Carolin Oelschlegel, and "Cultural Change That Sticks" in *Harvard Business Review*, coauthored with Ilona Steffen and Caroline Kronley.

Jon attended Brigham Young University and graduated with distinction from Stanford University in 1954 with a bachelor of arts degree in economics. He obtained his master of business administration from Harvard University, where he was a Baker Scholar, in 1959. Jon also served in the navy during the Korean War as a lieutenant (jg) in the Pacific on the USS *Whetstone* (LSD 27) and on the USS *Nicholas* (DDE 449).

James Thomas is a partner with PwC's Strategy& based in Dubai, United Arab Emirates. He leads the Katzenbach Center in the Middle East. In addition to having a background in oil and gas strategy consulting, James has worked extensively with organizations across industry sectors and across Europe and the Middle East to understand and evolve their cultures in pursuit of their strategic goals.

His client project experiences, from culture diagnostic to behavior-based transformation programs, have enabled substantial codification and development of the Katzenbach methodology. James has also spoken and written extensively on the topics of culture, behavior, and leadership, including "10 Principles of Organizational Culture" in *strategy+business*, coauthored with Jon Katzenbach and Carolin Oelschlegel, and the report *A Culture of Success: Using Culture for World-Class Results in GCC Companies*, coauthored with Georges Chehade, Per-Ola Karlsson, and Jon Katzenbach.

James holds a bachelor of science degree from Durham University. He lives in Dubai with his wife, Sophie, and three children, Sebastian, Florence, and Theodore.

Gretchen Anderson is a director at the Katzenbach Center, where she works with client teams across the globe who are operating at the intersection of strategy and organizational performance. Gretchen has been developing expertise in this field since she joined Katzenbach Partners in 2003. In the fifteen years since, she has developed a global, cross-industry perspective on the complex relationship between individual motivation and organizational performance. She writes, speaks, and advises on these topics.

Gretchen has a doctorate in literature from Stanford University. She likes to claim that her graduate thesis, which focused on women poets in Greenwich Village, signaled her eventual interest in how each individual's work life evolves in response to his or her environment. As an undergraduate, she studied at St. Hugh's College at Oxford University and graduated summa cum laude from Middlebury College in Vermont. She currently lives in Baltimore, Maryland, with her two children, Jane and Calvin.

Katzenbach Center Community of Practice Biographies

DeAnne Aguirre is a partner at Strategy&, PwC's strategy consulting business, and the head of US and Mexico strategy consulting and the global leader of the Katzenbach Center. Based in San Diego, she has over twenty-seven years of client service experience. She has written extensively on the topics of organizational culture, teaming, leadership, and talent strategy, and her most recent co-authored research and articles include "10 Principles of Leading Change Management" and "Culture and the Chief Executive." DeAnne has a passion for how all industry systems—and healthcare systems in particular—require a delicate balance between the individual and the collective and how bold symbolic acts of leaders can make all the difference.

Reid Carpenter is a director at PwC and the US leader for the Katzenbach Center Global Leadership Team, based in New York City. She has fourteen years of experience working with clients and is coauthor of "How to Unlock the Full Potential of Diverse Teams" and the author of "How to Find and Engage Authentic Informal Leaders." She considers herself a natural, lifetime observer of groups—their norms, patterns, and values—and appreciates how the center's work allows her to educate others in this practice and to help organizations make daily life and work more meaningful for people.

Varya Davidson is a partner at PwC's Strategy& and represents Asia-Pacific on the Katzenbach Center Global Leadership Team. She has worked primarily in the energy, utilities, and resource sectors globally. She has been consulting for over twenty-two years. Varya's passion is working proactively with organizational cultures to unlock enterprise value and accelerate change. She believes boards and executive teams must inform their strategic choices with cultural insights to truly harness an organization's potential. Varya has authored multiple articles and reports including "How Starbucks's Culture Brings Its Strategy to Life" in *Harvard Business Review* and the *17th Annual CEO Succession Study: Australian Boards Leading the Way on CEO Succession.*

Diana Dimitrova is a member of the global leadership team of the Katzenbach Center and a Munich-based director with PwC's Strategy&. With a master's in economics and doctorate in psychology, Diana has a deep passion for advancing leadership consciousness toward more sustainability, diversity, mindfulness, and intrapreneurship. Diana has more than ten years' experience consulting with clients on their transformation journeys, with a special focus on digital, and has coauthored articles such as "Building a Digital Culture" and "The Rise of Wellcare."

Kate Dugan is a PwC manager and former Katzenbach Center fellow on a mission to rid the world of bad management. In her role in the Katzenbach Center, Kate aspires to develop and inspire the next generation of emotionally agile leaders. She is the author of "Teaming with Young Guns" and "What the Ironman Taught Me about Communicating Goals" and coauthor of "Virtually Alone: Real Ways to Connect Remote Teams," all in *strategy+business.* Kate enjoys learning about psychology and economics, which fuels her quest to improve human performance and effect large-scale behavior change. In her spare time, Kate trains for endurance sports, coaches a triathlon team, and advocates against animal cruelty.

Jaime Estupiñán is a New York–based partner at PwC's Strategy& serving clients in health care and across industries in strategy and operating model transformation. He has supported health clients in creating sustainable, consumer-focused models impacting health care for millions of consumers and writes frequently on this topic. An engineer by training, he did his doctorate research in design of orthopedic implants at the Cornell Hospital for Special

Surgery Program in Biomechanics. Jaime cares deeply about elegant approaches to complex problems and focuses on pragmatic, multicompetency solutions to align organizations to strategy. He is a native of Colombia and grew up in Brazil and has supported clients in Latin America and globally.

Amanda Evison is a director at PwC's Strategy&, a member of the Katzenbach Center Global Leadership Team, and a former Katzenbach Center fellow. She has more than ten years of experience helping clients achieve organizational coherence—the alignment of strategy, operating model, and culture needed to deliver top performance. She has a passion for new ideas that radically challenge the status quo and harness the energy of the organization to drive behavior change.

Kristy Hull is a director at PwC's Strategy& and a member of the Katzenbach Center Global Leadership Team. Based in Washington, DC, she has more than twenty years of experience working with clients and is the author or coauthor of "Getting to the Critical Few Behaviors That Can Drive Cultural Change," "Use Culture to Pave the Way for Change," and other articles. She loves to help clients figure out how to revitalize their organizational culture to both accelerate their strategy and inspire their people to excel.

Michelle Kam is an Australian-based partner at PwC's Strategy&. She has a doctorate in psychology and is passionate about leveraging her understanding of human behavior to provide clients with strategies to realize potential through people. Her primary focus has been on leading whole-organization transformations, defining the operating model, culture, critical capabilities, people, and performance required to support strategic intent. She has diverse experience across sectors, including education, financial services, retail and consumer goods, the public sector, airlines, media, utilities, and health care.

Per-Ola Karlsson is a Dubai-based partner with Strategy&. He has more than thirty years of consulting experience, including leadership experience such as serving as a board of directors member for Booz & Company and as leader of that firm's European business and global people and organization strategy business. He was a founding member of the Katzenbach Center and has been active in it ever since. Relevant published works include "The Value of Getting CEO Succession Right," *A Culture of Success: Using Culture for World-Class Results in GCC Companies*, and "Are CEOs Less Ethical Than in the Past?"

Paolo Morley-Fletcher is a coleader for the Katzenbach Center in Europe, part of the Global Leadership Team, and a director with PwC's Strategy&. As both a consultant and an executive coach, he has spent more than fifteen years advising leaders and organizations internationally on leadership strategy, culture evolution, and transformational change. Paolo believes today's world demands a shift in leadership consciousness and organizational culture, wherein leaders focus inward. Paolo's written work includes "Transforming Leadership: How to Reduce Fear, Create from Uncertainty, and Make a Difference in the World."

Carolin Oelschlegel, one of the longest-standing core team members of the Katzenbach Center, is a director at PwC's Strategy& in San Francisco. She believes that companies that constantly evolve and refine their corporate culture will outgrow their competitors and deliver market-leading shareholder returns. Carolin has more than fifteen years of experience in management consulting with global organizations. She coauthored "10 Principles of Organizational Culture" with Jon Katzenbach and James Thomas, which has become one of the most read articles ever in the magazine *strategy+business*. Carolin recently led the Katzenbach Center's comprehensive Global Culture Survey 2018.

Frédéric Pirker is a Munich-based partner with PwC's Strategy&. Frédéric has more than fifteen years of consulting experience and leads the organization strategy practice in Europe. He is a member of the Katzenbach Center Global Leadership Team and coleads the center's European activities. He focuses on organizational transformation and buildup, including operating model review, organizational design, culture evolution, capability development, and implementation. Frédéric serves clients in the areas of consumer and retail, industrial products, health, telecommunications, and automotive.

Roger Rabbat is a Beirut-based director with PwC's Strategy& and a member of the Katzenbach Center global leadership team. He has over ten years of experience in management consulting and three years of experience in the construction industry. Roger has led a number of culture change and change management programs in the Gulf Cooperation Council and through this experience has built a deep belief that such programs lie at the heart of transformation efforts happening across industries and sectors, and throughout the region overall.

Barry Vorster is a South Africa–based partner at PwC. He has more than twenty-five years of consulting experience and has been enmeshed in helping organizations within the ambit of human resources, organizational culture, HR technology, learning, and the future of work. His passion is organizational learning, and he is fascinated by the interplay among organizational learning, technology, and large-scale behavior change. He enjoys the challenge of supporting organizations to act their way into new ways of thinking and behaving and is currently working on an article on the culture element of technology transformations.

Alice Zhou is a manager at PwC, a former Katzenbach Center fellow, and a member of the Katzenbach Center core team. She is based in Philadelphia and has ten years of client experience. She believes strongly that culture, just like strategy and operating models, involves deliberate trade-offs and that an all-purpose "ideal culture" does not exist. Alice's published works include "Improving Company Culture Is Not about Providing Free Snacks" and "How to Harness Employees' Emotional Energy."

Berrett–Koehler
Publishers

Berrett-Koehler is an independent publisher dedicated to an ambitious mission: *Connecting people and ideas to create a world that works for all.*

We believe that the solutions to the world's problems will come from all of us, working at all levels: in our organizations, in our society, and in our own lives. Our BK Business books help people make their organizations more humane, democratic, diverse, and effective (we don't think there's any contradiction there). Our BK Currents books offer pathways to creating a more just, equitable, and sustainable society. Our BK Life books help people create positive change in their lives and align their personal practices with their aspirations for a better world.

All of our books are designed to bring people seeking positive change together around the ideas that empower them to see and shape the world in a new way.

And we strive to practice what we preach. At the core of our approach is Stewardship, a deep sense of responsibility to administer the company for the benefit of all of our stakeholder groups including authors, customers, employees, investors, service providers, and the communities and environment around us. Everything we do is built around this and our other key values of quality, partnership, inclusion, and sustainability.

This is why we are both a B-Corporation and a California Benefit Corporation—a certification and a for-profit legal status that require us to adhere to the highest standards for corporate, social, and environmental performance.

We are grateful to our readers, authors, and other friends of the company who consider themselves to be part of the BK Community. We hope that you, too, will join us in our mission.

A BK Business Book

We hope you enjoy this BK Business book. BK Business books pioneer new leadership and management practices and socially responsible approaches to business. They are designed to provide you with groundbreaking and practical tools to transform your work and organizations while upholding the triple bottom line of people, planet, and profits. High-five!

To find out more, visit **www.bkconnection.com**.

Berrett–Koehler
Publishers

Connecting people and ideas
to create a world that works for all

Dear Reader,

Thank you for picking up this book and joining our worldwide community of Berrett-Koehler readers. We share ideas that bring positive change into people's lives, organizations, and society.

To welcome you, we'd like to offer you a free e-book. You can pick from among twelve of our bestselling books by entering the promotional code **BKP92E** here: http://www.bkconnection.com/welcome.

When you claim your free e-book, we'll also send you a copy of our e-newsletter, the *BK Communiqué*. Although you're free to unsubscribe, there are many benefits to sticking around. In every issue of our newsletter you'll find

• A free e-book
• Tips from famous authors
• Discounts on spotlight titles
• Hilarious insider publishing news
• A chance to win a prize for answering a riddle

Best of all, our readers tell us, "Your newsletter is the only one I actually read." So claim your gift today, and please stay in touch!

Sincerely,

Charlotte Ashlock
Steward of the BK Website

Questions? Comments? Contact me at bkcommunity@bkpub.com.

Certified

Corporation
bcorporation.net